My Mentor, My Guide

A Handbook for Daddies and Boys for the New Generation

Second Edition

Published by the Nazca Plains Corporation
Las Vegas, Nevada
2013

ISBN: 978-1-934625-45-3
E-Book: 978-1-61098-282-5

Published by
The Nazca Plains Corporation®
Paradise Rd, Suite 141
Las Vegas, NV 89109-8000

Cover, Fleshblack Images
Art Director, Blake Stephens

Dedication

I'd like to dedicate this book to you and to all those who are searching for something more.

A special thanks to my Leather family, the support of the local and international gay BD/SM Fetish community, my friends, the persons responsible for getting this book to you but most of all, to the young men I had the honor of calling my boys.

Lastly, as a tribute to the Mentors and Guides that made me the man I am today, I will always love them and never forget them.

My Mentor, My Guide

A Handbook for Daddies and Boys for the New Generation

Second Edition

Blade T. Bannon

Contents

Foreword

Thank you for taking the time to choose this book. I hope you enjoy reading it as much as I enjoyed the experience of putting it together. The book was a labor of love and even though it started off very fast, it took much longer than expected to finish. But I believe all good things come in their own time, so even with all of life's adventures seeming to get in the way, I knew it would all come together at the right place and time.

Now for the big question, what drew you to this book? Are you looking for something? If you chose it in the hope of finding some answers then you're in the right place. For every book or place that you look always has a golden nugget of wisdom hidden somewhere inside. The trick is to have an open mind so you can find them when they present themselves. With that in mind, I'm going to tell you what you won't find in this book. If you're looking for some kind of how-to book about how to set up your own dungeon or how to use some easy come-on lines to score a date then you may want to keep looking. This book explains the deep core issues of male bonding in the BD/SM fetish setting.

So why did I write this book? I wrote it for a number of reasons, some were personal and others spiritual but mostly I wrote it for you. To offer you a new view on where our culture is heading and to offer a map to help navigate through treacherous waters as safely as possible. In these pages you'll find truths that will free you in ways you won't expect. I presented the information in a simple format and added some stories to make the reading more interesting. My goal is for you to be better able to fully enjoy your sexuality and understand how close the bonds run between two people when respect, trust and understanding are present.

As for me I'm always looking for answers. I'm always changing and always growing. I believe that you never stop evolving. There's always something new to learn or experience. Life just works that way. You can fight it or be an element of change. The choice is yours.

To the Circle of Fire;
those who have gone before,
those who are present,
and those who have yet to come.

*Don Miguel Ruiz – The Four Agreements

Chapter 1: Daddies and Boys

The Search

It goes back in history as far as we care to look. Spartan warriors had their whole life built around the concept of older male mentors taking a younger male under their care and tutelage for training in combat. It was also common to take them as lovers. The Spartans were greatly feared by their enemies because of their intense male bond and dedication to each other in battle.

Today, young men are attracted to older men for many of the same reasons, experience, maturity, stability, the list goes on. However, in this day and age, it's easy to find sex anywhere without any meaningful bond. It's common and many do it because sex can be so easily separated from love or emotion.

It's as if sex has become just a mechanical act in order to get to a climax. In this modern age of technology, you just get on the computer and "order in," so to speak. If that's what you want, and that's all you're in it for, great. For many men, this works just fine; sex is very enjoyable and convenient. The idea of a meaningful bond is of no importance or simply forgotten.

However, in the sexual arena of the BD/SM lifestyle, there's much more that goes into it than a simple staged scene or mechanical act. I'm talking about something more meaningful, male bonding at its deepest levels. The type of bonding that carries the values and traditions of the past. These are life-changing experiences that bring men closer and make them stronger.

I remember when I was in my 20's and early 30's; I was always attracted to older, masculine men because they were more mature and were very good to me when we went behind closed bedroom doors. Now I've discovered I'm that guy! It's funny, but one day you wake up and become one of the men you once admired and respected. So boys, this one's for you.

Pick your Daddy wisely!

So how do you choose a Daddy? Good question, and I hope some of these answers will help you in making the best choice. After all, it's all about the boy. Most people don't get that part so I'll explain it in more detail a bit later. But for now let's look at Masters, Daddies, Trainers, Sir's, Mentors, Guides or whatever you decide your relationship to be. Even though the intensity and format of the relationships vary a great deal, their foundations remain the same.

The foundations are simple but not easily found and often need to be earned; communication; honesty; trust; commitment; compassion; integrity; imagination; tolerance; acceptance; inspiration; a high level of selflessness or love; and, in many cases, a deep level of spirituality of some kind. There's more, but let's just go with these for now.

While I'm at it, I'm also going to tie in the title of this book and why it relates to these qualities: Mentor, meaning teacher; and Guide, meaning way shower. As with all teachers, they've studied and often mastered the material in question prior to teaching. A Guide or way shower is someone who knows the territory and has already been down the path. Thus, "My Mentor, My Guide". No matter what formal title you bestow on him, or in some cases her, a Mentor or Guide will embrace many of these qualities because they've found that they produce the deepest bonding experiences. With that in mind let's get started.

Communication

Have you heard the old phrase, "communication is the key?" Well this is the BD/SM world, the word KEY is capitalized.

So, let's talk about the importance of communication. As much as we would like to read minds from time to time, we can't.

So the next best thing is open communication. The most seasoned Mentors will interview a potential trainee before making a commitment to take them under their wing. They want to get into the potential's head and see what motivates them or what their motivation is. Everyone comes into this for different reasons, but whatever they are, they're important.

By the way, communication isn't always about talking.

The most important part is being an active listener. "Active Listening" requires a good deal of skill, because it involves not only listening to the spoken word, but also tone of voice and body language. If you can master this skill, you can learn more about what a person is saying than they often realize themselves. Here's a little advice to the boys: if you want something, you need to communicate it. The same is true if you don't want something. Depending on the intensity of the play, it could mean the difference between a trip into sexual nirvana or to the hospital. How is this? In the BD/SM world, the words "no" or "stop" don't mean the same thing as they do in everyday life. Many times they mean just the opposite. Any experienced Guide or Mentor worth their weight in salt will have his trainee come up with a "safety word" before they explore any kind of play that could take the boy past any threshold he may not be able to handle. There are many thresholds and not all of them are about pain. I've seen boys damage themselves without being in any pain and not even know they've been injured. Safety words come in all shapes and sizes. If someone is gagged, then they'll have to come up with something else, for example, a "tap signal." That's why the Mentor has a huge responsibility in monitoring everything that's going on during a play session.

This reminds me of one of my boys, Carlo. He was well adjusted and highly educated. Carlo was also an excellent communicator. I recall a play session we had. He mentioned earlier in the week that he never knew his father and was never held by him as a child and told he was loved. He deeply wanted this as part of his male bonding experience. During our play session, I had him tied up and demanded he scream louder and louder as I worked him into a climax. He spent many years forcing himself to be quiet during sex, and now I was encouraging him to get reacquainted with a vocal climax.

Carlo was very nervous but obviously loving it at the same time. By the time he climaxed, I could see he was physically spent from our session but I knew I had one more thing to do.

I wrapped my arms around his naked, trembling body and lightly whispered in his ear, "Your Daddy loves you very much," and held him while he collapsed in a flood of tears on my chest. He was safe in my arms and was given the opportunity to let out his bottled up feelings. As the old saying goes, "If it's inside, let it out." Carlo and I became very close, and much healing came from our time together. We explored many of his fetish interests and his intellectual pursuits. Just the same, it wouldn't have been possible if he didn't communicate what he wanted.

Remember to always communicate what you want and don't be afraid to appear weak. It's by exposing your weaknesses and wants that a Mentor can guide you through any healing that can take place. Old wounds are mended and each person walks away stronger and more at peace with themselves.

Honesty

Now there's a big word, but what you're looking for is very simple. You're looking for someone who's honest from the start. How else can you build trust? I'll give you a good example. When I first meet with a potential trainee, I let them know I've been HIV positive for almost as long as they've been alive. I immediately set the stage with a foundation of honesty and trust. Now let's look at it from a different point of view.

Would the potential trainee have felt the same if I told him I was positive after our first sexual encounter even though we played safely? I think you get the point. Even if it isn't HIV, there are many STDs out there where some honesty beforehand would make a big difference. A Mentor needs to be honest right from the start. If you don't like what he's about, then you can move on, because the right one is just around the corner.

You might as well save both of you the time and effort. This goes both ways. Be honest with the Mentor from the start.

A real Mentor's core is about acceptance, so you want to be honest with him. He's going to find out the truth about you at some point anyway, so you might as well let him know right from the start. You want someone you can confide in. So let it out. By the way, this doesn't mean you're going to tell your whole life story on the first date either. Just the important stuff as it comes up will do just fine. Honesty builds trust. It also opens the door to the wonderful road of discovery, a road which you travel together.

Trust

Trust, now there's a good one. There have been many books written on the subject, all of which are very meaningful.

However, as my mother used to say "Keep it simple, Sweetie." With that in mind, trust is simply something that's earned by following through on what you say. Trust builds incredible strength in the relationship between the Mentor and his trainee. As trust grows the trainee will be more willing to explore more risky adventures and know he will be safe and protected by his Mentor or Guide. However, the Mentor needs the same follow through from the boy. If either of them does not feel they can be trusted or trust in the other, then they will have no foundation to work with and therefore end up with two possible courses of action. One is to sever the relationship which is never something to look forward to. The other is more positive and a great way to have fun and rebuild weakened trust. I'll get to this later when I talk about "Tolerance." Until then, I've often described trust as an emotional bank account.

Every time you break a promise to your Mentor or boy and don't follow through with someone you love, it's like taking a withdrawal from their emotional bank account. Their "trust" account so to speak. What happens when you keep taking withdrawals and make no deposits? One day you arrive to find the account is empty and the person gone. I often say, "Make deposits often, they add up fast." After all, trust is the mortar that holds everything together. Besides, making deposits is a lot of fun. No matter if they're big or small, deposits always count.

Commitment

Commitment goes hand-in-hand with trust. Once again, you need to follow through on your promises. It also means hanging in there when things aren't running smoothly. You need someone you can rely on not only when things are great but mostly when you need someone to talk to in times of hardship. I can't count how many times I've had boys call me after a very bad day and ask just to be with me for a while. All they wanted was someone they could feel safe and comfortable with. Everyone wants to know someone's in their corner. Someone who's not going to abandon them at the first sign of trouble.

However, a Mentor is a "Guide" not a rescuer. As someone once said to me, "Why do we fall down? So we can learn to pick ourselves up." Sometimes, it's knowing when to step back and let the boy make his own mistakes. The Mentor or Guide is the one who's there to brush off the dust after the fall and give the trainee the reassurance to pick themselves up, learn from it and move on. Commitment is being there, but only when appropriate. It's being committed to the relationship in whatever form you've built it.

Compassion

Compassion is another concept with many facets. However, I'm only going to focus on the aspects that relate to Mentoring and being trained. So let's begin with the fact that you need to get out of your own head space in order to express compassion for another.

Try and feel from their point of view. After all, their perception is their reality. This requires patience, but the rewards are beyond words. I have to admit, no one can fully know exactly how someone else is feeling, but we often have experienced something similar in the past to draw from. For a Mentor who's older than his boy, this comes much easier than for someone with less life experience. Maybe that's why you see so many pairings with a slight gap between the ages. The Mentor will often be able to say, "it's going to be alright, I've been through something like this before," and have a story to share if needed. Responding in this manner brings the two closer together by presenting common ground to stand on.

Even if there is no common ground to draw from, you have to try and understand by asking questions. This reminds me of a visit from my boy Brad (Pup) who was having a bad day at work and wanted to come and see me. I could tell by the tone of his voice that this visit was very important to him, so I agreed without hesitation. When he arrived, I escorted him to the back yard where he stripped off his clothes and got in the pool. I followed suit and asked him what happened at work. Pup was not one for words, so it came as no surprise when he retold the events of his day; he was very vague. His body language obviously stated that he wasn't finished, and I knew there was something more. I asked what else was bothering him. After a long pause, he really opened up and let it out. Someone he loved dearly was ill and lost his job at the same time. We talked about it, and I assured him that it's normal to feel frustrated when the people we love are going through hard times. Everyone goes through hard times at one point or another, but it only makes us stronger when we come out the other side. After he finished, he asked me to hold him.

Quite surprised, I agreed and drew him into my arms. After a moment, I asked him if he was "ok?" He nodded in agreement, then, like magic, he returned to his former self. The storm had passed and the clouds had parted. He just wanted someone to confide in. Sometimes it's just that easy, "sometimes." This goes for the boys as well. Daddies, Masters, Sirs, Mentors and Guides have bad days too and need some TLC, even if it's just giving them some time alone. Just remember, people are complex creatures so never assume anything. It's always a good idea to always ask questions for clarification. For now, just remember to try and see things from outside your point of view. Look for common ground regarding the situation. If there isn't any, ask questions for clarification about what the other person is feeling. Compassion is centered in a willingness to listen and an openness of heart.

Integrity

Now here's one that often leans heavily on the Mentor or Guide. Everyone wants the Daddy, Master, Sir, or whoever's in the dominant role, to have integrity. It seems anyone in a role model position is expected to have some level of integrity. The catch twenty-two is the huge range of meanings society has placed on this word. Once again, let's keep it basic. The first thing I'd like to point out is, integrity is everyone's responsibility.

It's making the right choice during difficult times. Not the easy one. People choose the easy road rather than sticking to what is right for the situation since doing what's right is more difficult or less fun. So often we see people going for what's easy or the "BBD – Bigger Better Deal." That's why integrity is so valued. Why is it everyone's responsibility? Because if you're always relying on someone else's integrity, then you're not holding yourself personally accountable for own. It's the old cliché of "passing the buck." No-one gets off in this category. If a boy is looking for a daddy with integrity then he must realize the daddy will be looking for a boy with the same potential.

I'll give you a simple example of making the right choice and using my personal integrity. One day I had made two dates. One was in the morning and one was in the afternoon.

The morning appointment was with an old friend I enjoyed going to the gym with. I helped him every day because he had many health problems and could openly share them with me.

He also liked the fact that I would always try and push him to do better, but I respected his boundaries when he was having a bad day. On this particular day, I got a call from one of my favorite boys. He offered to take me out to breakfast before he went to work. I knew this was a big deal for him because he was saving his money for a big trip but wanted to treat me anyway. "What to do?" I knew breakfast sounded like more fun than the gym; however, my friend was counting on me. I told the boy I already had plans to go to the gym even though my gym partner had usually called me by now. He understood and we ended the call. I knew he was disappointed because he didn't get the chance to go out with me very often, but I had to do what was right. I couldn't blow off my work-out partner.

Not two seconds later my phone rang and it was my workout partner. He said he was having a bad day and couldn't make it. I asked if he was alright and he assured me he was fine but just didn't feel up for the gym. He felt very bad about cancelling, but I quickly reassured him everything was alright.

We rescheduled for later in the week and said our goodbyes.

As soon as we were done, I called the boy and let him know breakfast was a go. I went to the gym after we ate and still met my afternoon appointment with plenty of time to spare.

You'd be surprised. Many things in life have a way of working out all by themselves. Just remember, even if they don't work out, stick to what is right rather than what is easy, or the BBD. You'll be well respected by the people in your life, and – more importantly – by yourself.

Imagination

Imagination is the most playful part of being a Mentor or a boy. This is where the magic happens. It's the well-spring of life and the Fountain of Youth. Haven't you heard the old saying, "Keep the child in you alive and playing"? Many boys seem to grasp this concept and run with it much more easily than the Daddies.

After all, the Daddy has to set an example; he has to be serious and responsible. The big question is, "is being serious all the time any fun?" I honestly think there's some unwritten law out there that says that "boys are always allowed to have fun and be playful." The great thing is they often remind the Daddies who like to play "The Heavy" to lighten up once in a while. As for me, I had too many wonderful years as a boy, so I refused to let go of my playful side.

So how does playful tie into imagination? Well, I guess the best way to describe this would be to share an experience I had with one of my boys. This boy's name was Brett, but I called him "Balloon Boy Brett." As you can tell from his nickname, Brett's fetish was balloons. Luckily I had the good fortune of having some previous experience with balloon play from a good friend of mine named Buster. On the other hand, I still had reservations since balloon play wasn't my fetish. Most of my problem was the fact that I wasn't being open minded and using my imagination in order to come up with some good ideas to incorporate his fetish into our play time. This boy was very special in the fact that he had incredible playful energy and a great imagination. So I asked him what types of things he'd like to explore with balloons. At first, we came up with fantasies together, then after I got a better feel for it, I was able to use my imagination to its fullest extent and come up with some real hot ones. All Brett needed was to have an inflated balloon pressed against his body in some erotic area or another and he was off and running. I'll share one play session with you to give you an idea.

One afternoon, I told Brett I wanted to fill a room full of balloons, throw him naked, and totally dominate him. Two days later, I came over for one of our usual play sessions and opened his bedroom door to find it had been filled ceiling to floor with balloons! I grabbed Brett, tossed him in, and quickly followed behind as balloons escaped into the living room. As I shut the door behind me, I heard the muffled pop as one of the last tried to escape. Balloons touched every part of my body as I swam through the room. I could hear them rustle and feel them vibrate as I moved along. My clothes came off in a trail as I went. It seemed all the furniture was removed from the room except the bed, and that's where I found Brett.

He was lying naked with a raging hard-on. I pounced on him like a panther on the hunt. I worked his nipples so hard he began to pre-cum then instructed him to keep his hands behind his head while I went down on him. I worked his cock hard and enjoyed watching him squirm on the bed while the cloud of balloons rustled all around us. One thing led to another, and soon we were covered in sweat which made the balloons steamy and slippery. Occasionally I would reach for one and pop it, but sometimes they would get away with a squeak of protest. At the end of the scene, we found ourselves in each other's arms, exhausted and satisfied. Just the same, Brett had one last request for me. He asked me to take out my knife and help him pop all of the balloons.

We then released what little pent up energy we had left by playfully emptying the room.

After we finished, we took a rest in the living room, but I had one more surprise for Brett. I dragged him back into the bedroom and dropped him on the bed. I then grabbed one of the largest balloons from his unused box and blew it up. Brett began to get excited as he watched and wondered what I was going to do to him. By the time the balloon was fully inflated, Brett was hard again. I instructed him to lie on his back with his legs hanging off the end of the bed. I then spat on his cock and slid the nozzle of the balloon over his rock-hard shaft. It fit smoothly and I could easily feel it throbbing through the latex.

I took my time working him up to a series of close climaxes before finally taking him over the edge. When he finally came, it exploded into the balloon with force, making a beautiful splatter pattern. What a work of art! I thought it would be a good idea to leave him with a souvenir, so I waited a moment then slowly pulled it off. When I knotted the stem a beautiful blossom of cum emerged from its tip. What do you think I did with that?

If you came up with an answer to my last question, then you'll have an easy time in this category. Just remember, the key was boy Brett. It didn't matter how much I liked his fetish but rather his ability to pull me into his fantasy. Watching him get turned on and charged up had an incredible sexual energy.

The mutual sexual energy we exchanged was intoxicating. After a while, the balloons just became part of the scenery. They became just an element in order to reach our real goal. Had I not been open minded and used some imagination, I would've missed out on one of the best experiences of my life.

Tolerance

Someone once told me, "Tolerance means putting up with a lot of other people's crap!" I don't know about that; I think of it more like, "Tolerance means understanding a lot about other people's issues." I get the impression the first one says you're willing to let people walk all over you, because you'll tolerate their behavior and just get mad about it. The second says you understand other people's issues but make a conscious decision to laugh about the situation and not let it get to you.

You can be present but not play into their game. This requires discipline on your part, but it will save you many headaches in the long run. Sometimes the Mentor has to use a great deal of tolerance when he's decided to take on a boy who's much less experienced or younger than himself. This one's for the Masters, Daddies, Sirs, etc.; "You chose them, so you need to let them be their age no matter how they act." Heck, some of the trouble I've seen boys get into makes me laugh, and age had nothing to do with it. Some stunts make no sense at all even when they're honestly trying to stay out of harm's way. From this view, tolerance is actually very comical.

It's also playful when you flip it back on someone. I'll share a little story about my boy Raphe and how this applies.

The comedy started right from the first night. I asked him to meet me at a local Leather bar. I wanted to expose him to the local Leather culture and let him know he was safe by my side. Raphe was instructed on what to wear, what time to show up, and – most of all – to wait at the door until I came out to get him. I got to the bar an hour early. I advised the doorman about Raphe and to let me know when he arrived. In the meantime, I went inside and visited with some old friends. I told them about Raphe so they stuck around to check him out.

Tolerance point number one: Raphe was late. He wasn't late just five minutes, not even 15. Try 30 minutes. When the doorman came and got me, the first words out of his mouth were that my boy was "in big trouble."

"I know he's late," I replied, but he said it was something else.

"He's wearing cologne." That was point number two. I made a big sigh and shook my head. That was one thing I took for granted and forgot to mention to him.

This was definitely not his fault. Luckily I had some leather-scented oil and quickly corrected the situation when I walked out to meet him. I also addressed the issue of his tardiness without hesitation. He offered a weak excuse, which I made a mental note of, then brought him in to meet everyone. The night went very well. However, over the weeks that followed, Raphe always had a knack for being late. I'd asked him about it but never seemed to get a viable excuse. So I came up with a way to flip this on him and have some fun teaching him the importance of being punctual at the same time.

Raphe desperately wanted to ride on a motorcycle as well as experience his first dungeon scene. I decided he would get both in the same day. I told him to be out at the curb in front of his place at exactly 4:00 pm. I would send someone by to collect him and take him to his first dungeon. This person would be in full leather and riding a motorcycle. Raphe's eyes lit up! I told him if he wasn't at the curb when the bike arrived then he would be out of luck. No exceptions. After all, other people's time was just as important as his. For the first time, that boy was punctual! As a matter of fact, he later confessed he was out at the curb 10 minutes early. Now comes the fun part. Would I be the type of Daddy who would send the pick-up person a bit late to have some fun with the boy and make a point?

As for the rest of the story, let's just say the three of us had an Earth-moving experience in the dungeon! It was a once in a lifetime event that sent him right over the top. As for Raphe's punctuality, he was never late again, and he always got a smile on his face whenever our eyes met from across a crowded room.

Tolerance requires you to understand other people's issues and make a conscious decision to laugh about the situation and not let it get to you. As with Raphe, you can offer guidance but that's all. Sometimes the guidance works and sometimes it doesn't. You still need to accept them for who they are.

Acceptance

Acceptance is a big one for me. We hear so much about diversity and acceptance in our community. Just face it, there's a flavor out there for everybody, so what's the big deal? People wanted diversity in this day and age; they got it. So let's get one thing straight: acceptance begins with you. Change the way you think and the world around you will change. How often have you heard about a straight person who said "I don't like homosexuals" until they were friends with one without knowing it? After he/she found out the so-called "horrible truth," it wasn't such a big deal. Then their view changed to "Some gays are alright I guess." Just because someone isn't your cup of tea doesn't mean judging them is the answer. They just want to live their life.

All of us want to live our lives and be happy. It's a pretty simple concept really. If what they're doing is bothersome, then speak up and let them know. It's just like a family member getting on your nerves. You simply let them know and move on. Just make sure you look into your own motives before ever making a comment or you may end up being the person who's out of line. Everyone has a particular group they feel more comfortable with, usually because of common interests and beliefs. It's "ok" to be separate; however, it doesn't make anyone better than anyone else. The point here is: "Let's just have fun with each other."

Sometimes we're working so hard on acceptance and unity in our community that we don't stop to see how far we've actually come. I remembered being honored as one of the Emcees at the 2006 Southwest Leather Pride and Leather title holders' competition. As I looked out into the crowd, I saw representatives from every branch of our diverse family tree.

What really made me smile was each group came up on stage and helped raise money for the event and charity. Now that's what I call unity in the community! How does this relate to the Mentor and his boy? It's simple.

Just like differences between interest groups in our community, Mentors and their trainees will sometimes differ on what they like to explore. This doesn't mean a mismatch. The Mentor or Guide has two choices: (1) be current on the boy's fetish, or (2) introduce someone experienced to the trainee who the Mentor completely trusts. Just because something isn't in the Mentor's bag doesn't mean the boy should be robbed of the experience.

Remember Balloon Boy Brett? This is an opportunity for growth and exploration. The boy also has to keep in mind that the Guide may need to have a "get away" weekend once in a while to explore something the boy isn't interested in, or something too extreme for him to deal with. It's sometimes nice to add a third person into the mix to bring some new energy to the situation. Some of the best bonding can occur with more than two, so don't restrict yourself.

Sometimes our differences are hard to accept, because it's something we don't like or agree with. Keep an open mind and ask questions. Acceptance comes from understanding a person "beyond" what you assumed you knew about them.

Many times you'll be pleasantly surprised to find some new discoveries about both them, and most importantly, about yourself.

Inspiration

Inspiration… what a wonderful word. The power to inspire or be inspired is one of the greatest gifts a person can give to another. How often have you read a book or seen a movie that moved you deeply? Now think of a person who inspired you.

Sometimes it's someone you've never met. This is the power and the gift of inspiration. Inspiration is such a strong force because it changes people and the way they think; its greatest facet is its ability to promote action and cause change. The changes may happen to the world around us or, in many cases, they may occur within us. The most remarkable thing about it is that everyone has the opportunity to inspire others. The big question is, "Have we been taking advantage of this opportunity?" Being a Mentor or Guide puts a person in the spotlight for inspiring those who they take under their wing. I have been forever changed by those who guided me. I hold them in the highest regard and respect. They made me the man I am today.

So for those boys looking for a Daddy and asking, "How do I know what inspiration looks like and how will I know it when I see it?" I'll give you a way to define it more clearly.

Simply put, it's someone who supports your interests and dreams. How many times have you seen someone inspired to do something only to have someone talk them out of it by explaining all the road blocks and pitfalls that "could" happen before they even start?

Now a bit of advice for the Daddies: Even if you know from past experience that your boy's subject of interest is not going in the best direction, you still need to practice patience. You can share a story as a point of reference in order to guide, but remember to always support them. Everyone has to learn for themselves. Mentors who inspire, support others in their interests and dreams. It doesn't matter if it works out in the end. The fun is in the journey. Besides, if it doesn't work out, it becomes a great learning experience just the same.

Remember that inspiration brings people together and creates strong emotional bonds. This is one of the many gifts of inspiration. The reason it's such a strong force is because it promotes action and has the ability to change the world around us.

A High Level of Selflessness or Love

Many have said Love and the gift of selflessness are truly presenting your higher self. The big questions are, "How does one achieve this?" and "What path does one take?" Let me just say that everyone's path is different, and it's up to you to find it.

However, I do have some experiences regarding my path that may shed some light on the topic and offer some guidance so you know what you're looking for. For me, the journey began by learning to deeply love myself. After all, how can you give others what you don't have for yourself? I read through volumes of psychology books to find the answers.

It's funny, but in high school, they teach math, English, history, etc., but never the most important things: how to love yourself and how to treat others lovingly. When you get into college you have detailed psychology, but in many cases it's very clinical, sterile, and analytical. Today's world is very different. When once there was philosophy and poetry, now there are scores of books on the subject of love and how to express it. One good look at any Mentor's library and you'll know the direction of his reading interests. However, never assume his bookshelf tells his story; life experience counts just as heavily as books. If you don't practice or share what you've learned in life, have you really learned anything?

Knowing yourself and loving yourself is a life-long journey.

By taking this path, you become more willing to open up and express who you are to others. People around you pick up on this and feel safe to be open in your presence. They feel safe around you, because they know you're "authentic." I'm not saying this will happen all the time. As I mentioned before, this isn't a perfect world and many people can't let go of their past or their fears of being hurt.

Just the same, some Mentors or Guides will be looking for a boy who has started this journey. He knows the one he chooses will have the capacity to look into all those deep inner places. The places they'll be going together.

Now, for the boys looking for a Daddy, once again you're asking, "What do I look for?" First of all, being selfless in a loving manner takes a great deal of self-control and restraint. I'll keep it simple by sharing more life experiences with you.

For example, I've been happily partnered for 13 years and I've mentored roughly a dozen boys. All of these men came into my life HIV negative and still are today. I started having sex just before AIDS came into the world. I know how enjoyable unsafe sex is and I loved the intimacy it creates.

However, I love the people in my life much more than the risk of harming them. There have been so many times when I had to practice restraint in order to do what was best, especially when my HIV negative sex partner wanted otherwise. One of the greatest gifts of the BD/SM lifestyle is that sex doesn't revolve around intercourse. It's just one of the many roads we take into intimacy. A Daddy worth something will always want to do what's best for your safety and well-being. Daddies that give you an impression of a protector or guardian without being overbearing are a good choice.

Remember to start by loving yourself. The deeper the self-love, the more you'll be able to give to others. Being selfless is not draining, because you're giving it willingly. After all, you've got plenty of love to spare, since love is infinite.

A deep level of spirituality of some kind.

This is something most people get very emotional about because it touches our deepest beliefs. So I want to talk about a few things before I get into spirituality. First of all, there are many times when religion overlaps or donates to spirituality but they are not the same from my point of view. I have traveled all over the world and been exposed to many religions. I have found the same great truths in all of them. It's like the spokes of a great wheel. They are the same in their central goal to achieve a better understanding or personal relationship with the Divine and to attain enlightenment. However, each has a different path getting there. I'll go into more detail regarding spirituality a bit later but for now let's get back to Mentors and their boys.

So, once again you're asking, "How does this relate to boys searching for a Daddy?" Again the answer is simple. You want to look for a Mentor/Guide who's at peace with himself and God as he sees him/her, even if he/she does not believe in any form of God. This is especially true in relation to his sexuality. Most religions aren't too accepting of homosexuality as they're taught in childhood. It takes a while to work things out and once again be at peace with ourselves and the Divine.

Many people have been spoon fed their faith as a child. You're an adult now and you can distinguish between the irrational material and what brings you inner peace. The Daddy who's asked himself these questions has put himself on a different path. He'll be more at peace with himself and his sexuality.

It's not a mandatory item on the Daddy list but it sure helps if he doesn't have conflicting voices in his head regarding his actions.

Now you may be thinking, "Wow, I think I've got a better idea of what to look for." Good, but just remember Mentors come in all shapes and sizes. They're stronger is some suits more than others. Some of the things I've mentioned may be important to you, others may not. It's up to you to decide which will be your best match.

Chapter 2: Pitfalls and Traps

"Coming out in the BD/SM World"

Why are pitfalls and traps important? Because as much as I believe it's a beautiful and perfect world, there are people out there with hidden agendas that are far from what you're looking for. I don't consider these people as "bad" just a product of their life experiences, or in some cases, a lack of them. My intention is not to scare you but rather to enlighten you. Everyone falls into traps because traps are always cleverly disguised. Even with the most honorable of intentions it's easy to get caught in one. Sometimes it just makes sense to let you know what these scenarios are because they're easier to avoid. I'll give you some examples of what I've come across in my travels. In some cases, I'll share a story to go along with it, in others I'll just give you a description. Either way, I hope they provide you with a map to guide you safely around any potential mine fields and into greener pastures.

Posturing Tops

The first type I'd like to visit is the most common. I refer to them as the "Posturing Tops." I often get the impression of these individuals as all puffed up and always putting on a performance rather than being themselves. One thing I hear over and over again regarding these types is coercion. Some big Leather Top finds some new, inexperienced boy and tells him he isn't a real Leathermen unless he does this or that. The "this or that" is usually the hollow needs of the Top, who just wants to use the boy for his momentary gain, at the boy's expense. What usually follows is the boy walks away from the experience feeling used or unfulfilled, except for the fact that he's proven himself as "making the grade." How does this happen? The Top will act the part and look so irresistible to the boy that he doesn't want to pass up the opportunity, or the Top has been around a while and knows how to drop names to impress the boy. These types use their status to define who they are and the boy is just an extension of their image. Even though this doesn't sound good, it does work for some and I've seen male bonding result from it. Some boys like to be in the spotlight and love to be exhibitionists. What better way to meet at least one of their needs? I just wanted you to be aware and ask yourself, "Is this what I want?"

Pretenders

Another category is what I call "The Pretenders." These guys act like they have experience but don't. They sure look the part but can really mess you up. In your travels you may hear about what was once called the Old Guard. Unfortunately, most of them have respectively passed away. Father Time and AIDS took their toll. It's a sad thing too. Much of our valuable BD/SM knowledge was passed down from one man to another, "Daddy to boy", over the years. A huge break was made in the chain of knowledge because of AIDS. There are some of us that lived through it and were trained by some of the last of the Old Guard but even we are different in our thinking. After all, every generation puts its own timestamp on the training as they pass it along. However, the Pretenders are a whole different breed. These guys never mentored under anyone and are self-proclaimed Tops. They've read a book or two which, if they're lucky, gives them just enough knowledge to make them dangerous. Many find the porn they watch is the way they run their real life play scenes. They're the most likely to put you in the hospital or leave you with a permanent mark you weren't planning on. However, in their defense, some go to play parties and learn by tag-team toping with someone experienced. Just remember, their experience only extends as far as the amount of hands-on play they've had. So if you plan on choosing a Daddy that never had a boy, I strongly suggest you find out if he's got a lot of hands-on experience. If he doesn't, then think about it before you make a decision regarding any heavy play.

GDIs, or Loose Cannons

This next type is interesting: God Damn Independents, otherwise known as GDIs or Loose Cannons. They're why it's so important for someone entering the lifestyle to have a guide. After all, when I first started, I was a GDI. I wanted it all. I thought I could handle myself and didn't want to be weighed down by just one guy. I took martial arts as a matter of self-preservation and eventually became an instructor. After all, I didn't want some big Daddy overpowering me. I was a real tough guy, yeah right. Looking back, martial arts did help me, though not in the ways I expected. Most situations required the right Daddy, and I didn't really know what I was looking for. All I wanted was someone who was masculine and looked hot. Isn't that what every young and ambitious boy wants?

So I started out as a free agent. I think a better term for me would be "Loose Cannon on the deck!" I was someone with something to prove and the old "I'll-show-you" attitude. Back in those days, it was known as "cocky." I was also very impatient.

This attitude usually brought out the worst in Old Guard Tops, because it was a blatant show of disrespect for their status in the community. This behavior always called for some level of discipline, and most of the time, it wasn't pleasant.

Speaking of Old Guard discipline reminds me of the first Leather competition I ever attended. During one of the afternoon events, I had the chance to sit with one of the Old Guard Tops named Raven.

He was silver-haired with a military style crew cut and a very short cropped beard, but still looked very hot for someone way out of my age range. He had his boy with him and shared a story about one of their recent sessions regarding discipline.

I became a sponge soaking up every drop of his story. He started by telling me he stripped his boy naked and hog-tied him on his belly. He made sure the boy could see everything he was doing. Then he took a pile of red hot coals and stuck a branding iron in them. After the iron was red hot, he placed a piece of raw chicken on the floor in front of his face. He then took the hot iron and thrust it into the chicken. He said he wanted the boy to smell the burning chicken and hear the crackle of the burning flesh. He then told the boy to prepare himself to be branded. He blind folded the boy, took an iron which was sitting in a bowl of ice and branded the boy's butt.

The boy jumped and screamed thinking he had been burned, since the sensation of hot and cold are so similar. Raven said he was surprised and excited to see the boy's ass swell up, because in his mind, he thought he had been branded. I, on the other hand, was totally freaked out. This kind of play was way past my limits as a beginner, and I didn't want anything to do with someone who "mind-fucks" like that. I marked him as dangerous and didn't want anything further to do with him.

Someone else less experienced than myself may have exited the patio never to return again. It's too bad. Had I known that the scene was consensual, I'd have known Raven would've stayed within my boundaries, and I could have learned a lot from him too.

However, the point here is that a GDI would most likely jump into a scene like this before getting all the details, because of the "I'll-show-you" attitude, or because the Top was hot and he just wanted to experience something new. This is how GDIs end up with an unwanted "mind-fuck" or, worse yet, a real branding. Often it's the GDIs or Loose Cannons, or in some cases the abuser, that end up the victim. Either way, you're now aware.

It's funny how very similar the GDIs and the Pretenders are, considering that neither starts out with any practical experience. Many carry a chip on their shoulders and are willing to try things beyond their experience level.

The difference is the pretenders will rarely admit their lack of experience because they're afraid they'll appear weak or undesirable. GDIs or Loose Cannons on the other hand, are just impatient and are often readily teachable if they can settle down long enough.

In my case, the only saving grace was the fact that I got involved in local Leather competitions early in the game. The reason this saved me is because I was able to associate with the Leather folk who cared about the community. People who wanted to inspire change. You could always tell the ones who really shined. They had a depth of character that drew you to them. I guess you could say they had a peaceful type of charisma. There was no doubt how they earned their titles and they managed to keep my impatient nature at bay.

Professional Victims

Speaking of victims, have you ever heard of a "professional victim"? Yep, they're out there and in large numbers these days. You'd think this would be a trap for a Daddy, but this one goes both ways. As I mentioned before, everyone falls into traps, because traps are always cleverly disguised. Even with the most honorable of intentions, it's easy to get caught in one.

Such is the case with professional victims. Daddy's and boys beware this one will blind-side you. I'll share a couple of life stories from both sides of the fence to give you an idea of how it works.

The first one is called "Baby Huey." It started as a triad relationship when a couple of Leathermen I know took in a boy they'd found. Shortly after move-in, one of the Daddies died. Unfortunately it was the more dominant partner of the relationship. The boy offered no support, emotionally or otherwise, to the remaining Daddy in the house. All he wanted was someone to put him up and pay all the bills. He figured he didn't need to do anything else as long as he kept playing the part. He never cleaned up after himself and made no effort to pitch-in unless threatened. This was difficult for the remaining Daddy because he relied on his partner to fulfill the disciplinary role. Matters slowly got worse, and he even came up with the name "Baby Huey" for the boy because he was such high maintenance. Debt agencies sent letters regarding his bills via mail and endless calls came by phone. My friend came to me for a way out. I remembered some of my Old Guard training and knew a bit of militant discipline would most likely do the trick, so I volunteered to collar and work with him. The kid had potential in the sexual arena, but he had no intention of taking any personal responsibility for his life. He made an excuse for everything. Why he couldn't find a job, even though he had all the resources to do so; or help out around the house and so on. Every time he made an excuse, he made himself out to be the victim. It was never his fault. He had no intention of doing anything because it was easier to let everyone else do it. Unfortunately, life doesn't work that way.

This boy grew very fond of me, and it crushed him when I took back his collar. He was the first boy I ever had to do it to. I sat him down and told him that there are certain lessons in life that have to be learned before you can go as deeply as I wanted to go with him. Taking responsibility for his life was one of them. I told him I would be willing to pick up from where we left off once he learned this lesson. I reassured him that he was a good person and someday, hopefully, he would be back for his collar. Until then I would be waiting.

I met with his live-in Daddy and advised him of the situation. I advised him to set up some boundaries or the boy would continue to walk all over him. He gave the boy a month to find a job or be out of the house. The boy thought he wasn't going to hold to his word and didn't look for a job. To this day Baby Huey drifts from Daddy to Daddy's house until they tire of his "professional victim" routine and force him to move on.

Other friends have referred to this as "taking in a stray dog or bird with a broken wing." Just the same, using a role to exploit someone for your own personal gain is not what I would call "presenting your higher self." How can you reach the deepest levels of trust with someone if they feel they're always being used or taken advantage of?

Now, how does a boy fall into this trap with a Daddy?

Once again I'll share a little story with you. I call this one "The boy with three Daddies." This boy had one Daddy that was his lover, soul mate and domestic partner. The second was his sex partner. I was the third, "The Leather, Mentor and Play Daddy." You could say it was an interesting set up, but it was stable and worked very well for everyone until a bad chain of events happened to Daddy number two. Among other things, the sex partner Daddy was between jobs and going through a bought of depression. The boy was prone to depression himself from time to time but had a good handle on it for quite some time.

That was until he made his Daddy number two's problems and depression his problem to fix. It didn't happen all at once. It happened little by little. First he offered moral and emotional support. Then he made it his task to get him a job because the Daddy was too depressed to do it and it went on from there.

Every time the Daddy would call saying he was depressed and felt suicidal, the boy would rush over to be with him. After a while the boy was emotionally exhausted and began to fall into a depression himself. I tried to offer some guidance in the matter but it fell on deaf ears. Eventually everything worked itself out but the boy went through a lot of unnecessary depression, pain and suffering. After all no-body's perfect, so you see how easy it can be to care for someone so much that anyone can find them self in a scenario like this.

My boy Carlo once told me something I'll never forget and I guess it sums up this whole situation. He said "Don't try and fix someone else's problems because it only makes them twice as hard to fix."

Rescuers

The Baby Hues boys and others like them seek out these people. The rescuer buys into whatever story is being fed to them and the next thing you know, they're handing over a spare set of keys to their place or over-expending their credit cards to help out. After all, they've got the best of intentions in helping a fellow human being get back on their feet and, in some cases, with the hope of scoring some sex in exchange for the helping hand. Sometimes it works out but most of the time they get stuck with the short end of the stick. However, the dangerous ones are the ones who try to control whoever enters their world. My good friend Chris took the time to share his story of just such a person. I call it, "The Story of Mr. X".

Mr. X met my friend out at one of the usual places and immediately started buying things for him. He doted over him endlessly and tried to make a big impression on him every time he got the chance. He soon convinced Chris it would be in his best interest if he moved in with Mr. X, so he could help him get his financial issues in order. Chris accepted. After all, Mr. X was giving him a well needed break on rent and living expenses.

After Mr. X had him in the house, he started to change. He insisted that Chris stay away from all of his friends because they were a bad influence. After all, it was his friends' fault for getting him in his current financial situation. The boy was quickly isolated and alone except for Mr. X. This went on for months, and Chris began to believe everything that Mr. X would tell him because he was constantly being emotionally beat down. He then insisted that Chris turn over all of his financial information because he was a former credit repair specialist, and he wanted to get right to work on his issues. He quickly put his name on all the accounts. Then one day Chris got lucky and took the advice of a friend who managed to get through just in time. He got away from Mr. X while he was out of the house but not without finding out something very disturbing while he was packing. It seems Mr. X had run up all his credit cards, destroyed all his credit, and taken out a very large life insurance policy on him. The boy also recalled Mr. X making a big deal about going away on a very important trip in the near future "alone".

Many rescuers have good intentions but some don't. The real question is: does anyone really need to be rescued in the first place? You can always rescue yourself. It's "ok" to ask friends for help, but it's up to you to clean up your own mess.

Everyone runs into rough patches in life. It's how you deal with them that makes the difference.

Accidental Drug Addictions

I prefer to say accidental drug addictions, because most people don't plan on becoming addicted to drugs or other substances. It happens because of other circumstances in their lives or, as I mentioned before, "by accident." They try it while out with some friends because they think it will be fun and then don't stop. However, I've never seen this one hit home so much and so deeply as it did in the generation of the late-90's into the 21st century.

When I was in my teens "pot" was the big drug of choice and that stuff only seemed to give you the munchies and make you lethargic. I refer to today's drug scene as the "Alphabet Club." There's X, G, K, and so on. The worst is Crystal Methamphetamine or Crystal Meth for short. I've seen so many lives totally destroyed by it and it happens very quickly. Now I'm not saying everyone who tries these things is doomed.

Many people have told me that they like to take X recreationally when going out clubbing so they can enjoy dancing all night, and I can understand where they're coming from. They used to tell me that about pot when I was a kid, but then again, Crystal Meth isn't pot, is it? When you look at it from the BD/SM sexual arena however, it takes on a whole new meaning.

In the BD/SM world the Holy Grail rules of play are "Safe, Sane and Consensual Sex." This seems to go right out the window when Crystal Meth or too much of any other recreational drugs enter the scene. Today you'll often have people ask you "Do you Party and Play?" or PNP as it's used on the Internet.

Sadly, there are actually terms for some of the sexual side effects of playing while on drugs. Terms like, "Crystal Dick" which in many cases means a guy can't get it up. What usually happens in a "play party" situation is the person turns into what some refer to as a "Power Bottom" and won't stop until he can get fucked by as many guys as possible. After all, his dick is out of order and his drug induced desire to have intense sex is very strong.

This is where the first of the three "Grail Rules" gets broken because someone in this state is too impatient to practice safe sex and will go "Bareback." Unfortunately, if he was HIV negative at the beginning of the night, chances are he wouldn't be by its end. As far as the other "Grail Rules" are concerned, they often go out the window while heavily under the influence of these substances. So if you are a beginner in the BD/SM scene, a word of advice would be to stay clear of people who like to Party and Play heavily. It's not that they are bad, but do you want to take any extra chances with someone who may not be in charge of all their faculties?

The addiction situations I've just mentioned are bad enough, but the worst by far is when you have a member of your Leather family fall into drug addiction. This reminds me of a couple of life experiences. The first was with one of my oldest and dearest friends named Terry. Terry was a fellow Leatherman and a bartender most of his life. He lived life fully, and even though he would drift in and out of my life, it was like no time was lost between visits. Unfortunately, Terry also had a bit of a problem with alcohol and drug use. One day I went over to his place to visit with him. Everything was fine and the conversation was relaxed. Then Terry asked to excuse himself for a moment because he wanted to "shoot up" and didn't feel comfortable doing it in front of anyone. I was a bit stunned by the way he was so matter-of-fact about the statement and didn't quite believe him at first so I asked if I could watch. I also wanted to get a better understanding of what the process was like and why someone would want to do it. He gave me a strange look but agreed. So off we went. He pulled out all of the materials to get started. The strange part about it was that we just continued to carry on our previous conversation while he went through the motions preparing his injection. Every once and a while, he would point out a safety feature he was performing to reassure me that he was being safe. He did mention at least two times that he had a handle on this, and that it was strictly recreational. I said, "Terry I honestly think you've gone past recreational use and are you going to get some help in dealing with it?" Terry assured me he was fine and jokingly said he'd call me from the detox center if he OD'd. Unfortunately, this wasn't Terry's first brush with going too far with recreational use, so I knew the chances were very good that his joke might be a reality. A month later I got a call from the detox wing of the hospital. It was Terry and he wanted a friend to talk to. He knew I wouldn't lecture him. What he really wanted was a friend to support him on his road back to sobriety. Terry's case was a mild one because he never really turned anyone else's life up-side-down with his addiction. I've seen some of the most honest people turn into the cleverest liars to get money to support their habit. I've visited one friend I didn't know had gotten hooked on Crystal who upon arriving found him with this apartment all dark, all the blinds drawn and tissue stuffed in all the cracks of the windows because he thought he was being watched. His pupils were so large you almost couldn't make out the color of his eyes. I have to admit it was pretty creepy to witness. The saddest part about all this is the friends who care so much that they'll try to save them and get dragged into the addict's mess.

I've heard of people getting ripped off by someone they were trying to help or worst yet almost lose their house or going to jail because the cops came over and found their friend's drugs.

The list goes on and I'm sure you've got stories of your own to tell. The saddest part of all this is most of these people in question had great lives with great jobs before this happened to them. That's what makes it all the more difficult to practice the fine art of detachment. At first it may seem cold, but it is necessary. You can care for someone deeply but still know that the best thing for them is for you to step back for a while and let them go through whatever it is that they're doing so it doesn't turn your world up-side-down. An old friend once said to me, "If you see you're standing in the path of a tornado, it's a good idea to get out of the way." I also added to this statement, "If you step out of the way, you'll be in a better position to help others left in the debris field." Just remember one thing: try and have some compassion for these individuals. After all, they're living in their own, self-created hell. From their point of view, they see what they're doing as totally justified and are often confused as to why things aren't working out the way they want. Just the same, there is a wonderful irony in all this. You will find many of the best Mentors or Guides are twelve step programs. I'll talk more about this in the next chapter. For now, just remember to have compassion and understanding. It makes detachment much easier.

Lonely Only

Then there are the poor souls that always need to be with someone. They believe their lives aren't meaningful until they find that special someone to complete them. This reminds me of when I was in my twenties. I used to laugh when I went out to the bars with friends and listened to them talk about their relationships or their desire for them. The ones that were in relationships envied the freedom of their single counterparts.

The singles, on the other hand, wanted the companionship of knowing they always had that "special someone" to come home to. No one seemed very happy with what they already had.

When someone asked me my view on being single and being in a relationship I'd simply say, "When I was married I was very happily married and when I was single I was very happily single." I always looked at the good points of each and enjoyed them whether I was in a relationship or single. After all, you really don't need anyone to "complete" you to be happy.

Now how does this apply to a pitfall or trap? Well, it's basically very simple. If someone comes into a Daddy/ boy, or any other relationship, because of a fear of being alone they run the high risk of becoming what some friends have referred to as an "Emotional Vampire." Their need for security and commitment becomes so great that they literally drain their counterpart of all of their creative energy, time, and freedom.

This leads their counterpart into feelings of being trapped and stifled. They'll begin to feel like they need to "check-in" with their partner when calling rather than just enjoying their conversation. In the end, they both feel drained, and after one, or both, hit their personal limit they part. Of course this further reinforces the need to be with someone, because of the feelings of abandonment and a failed relationship. Many refer to them as heavily codependent. These poor souls usually suffer from low self-esteem and can usually be identified by the way they respond to questions like, "How are you today?" Answer with an "I'm alone... I guess I'm not good enough to be with someone. If I could only find the right Daddy/Lover/boy, my life would be perfect. They'd fix everything! I don't like being or sleeping alone." They'll often go from one relationship to another with little or no time in between. Their compelling need to be with someone rather than being alone far outweighs any need for personal growth and development. They're trapped in a loop and don't know how to get out.

If this sounds familiar and you want to try and find a way out of this loop, then I'd like to share a little something from Marianne Williamson. She put it quite nicely in her lecture about intimacy. It went something like this:

"You know that list you make of the perfect partner? The one with all the qualities you want, like loving, caring, kind or fabulous, etc. Take a good long look at that list and then ask yourself something...Would they date you? And continue: It's not that they aren't there....YOU haven't shown up yet. Or if they have shown up they got bored, can you blame them?"

"Relinquish your focus on them."

"They're a vision implanted in your heart."

Now I want you to go back to that list and ask yourself something else: "What would be the perfect partner for this person?"

That's the list you need to focus on! First, look inward and change yourself. Get to know yourself and love yourself. It's the old law of attraction, "like attracts like." Then you'll be on a road that will bring better results.

It's amazing, but even those of us who have taken a great deal of time and care in learning to master the art of relating and loving sometimes fall into traps. Why? Because – as I mentioned before – everyone falls into traps, because traps are always cleverly disguised. Even with the most honorable of intentions it's easy to get caught in one. If you fall into one, it's okay, just pick yourself up and learn from it. The difference is knowledge, the knowledge to know better and choose more wisely in the next round. After all, we are the sum of our life experiences, so even the bad things are growth experiences and should be looked at as good and valuable.

Chapter 3: Mentors and Guides

What makes them Different?

What makes Mentors or Guides different? I found some common life experiences that Mentors and Guides share.

They seem to add to the depth of the person's character and promote those deep levels of bonding that I've been talking about. This isn't a full list by a long shot but a nice start. Sometimes a Mentor may have been exposed to only one of these experiences, though – in some cases – even more than that. I don't believe these trademark experiences are mandatory, but they're a nice indicator for someone who's looking.

For example, many Mentors haven't been dealt the best hand in life at one point or another but know it's how well you play out what you've been dealt that counts. With this in mind, let's get started on what some of these life experiences are.

Trial by Fire, or a test of one's personal steel, is a trademark of a good Mentor. This is someone who's already faced one of their biggest demons. I mentioned previously that 12-Stepper's make great Mentors. This is because they've had to face one of their greatest demons, whether it be alcohol or drugs. They've chosen to and take ownership of it.

Part of the process of going through the 12 steps is doing a personal inventory, any Mentor or Guide worth his or her weight in salt has taken on this task, looking inward and seeing what you're really about. This can be very difficult and painful for some, and I believe that's why so many shy away from doing it. However, there is no mistaking its importance. No matter how painful the thought of it may seem, the rewards of such a journey are well worth the effort. 12-Steppers have discovered this precious gift and strive to cultivate it in others through their example. Guiding by example and a "Live and Let Live" philosophy is by far one of the highest forms of mentoring. It is for this reason that seasoned 12-Steppers have such great value as Mentors or Guides.

Then there's the Adventure seekers. This group is easily misread as just adrenaline junkies, weekend warriors, or restless hearts. But a closer look reveals something much more powerful and profound. This group inhales the deepest essence of life by truly living in the moment. They take on some sort of extreme sport or physically demanding activity.

This takes them to the edge of their limits. It's something that demands all of their focus and attention. A good example of this is one of my boys Thomas (Tiger). He's a rock climber, owns a very successful landscape design business, and, as he likes to put it, "takes life by the horns." Tiger was over the other night, and we talked about his experiences when he's up there on the cliff face hanging on by just his fingertips.

He said there's nothing else like it, "It's a moment when you're not scared. It's like everything gets quiet and the world just goes away. It's just you and the cliff. It's very peaceful and I love that feeling." I understood what he was talking about, because I've run the gambit of extreme sports in my search to always return to that place. People who've found this path to inner-peace are easily hooked because of the duel high they get from the experience. The high of that moment as Tiger said "It's like everything gets quiet and the world just goes away" and the thrill of conquering a very grueling and painful physical challenge. If you're an adventure seeker, you understand what I'm talking about. As for me, after an unexpected illness which left me unable to do these things, I was told my days of extreme sports were over. I've since found less physically demanding ways to bring myself to this place of serenity. Oddly enough I still long for it, because like all adventure seekers, I know they remind me I'm fully alive and forever young at heart. Just the same, I'm like all adventure seekers and not a quitter.

So you see, these individuals make great Mentors or Guides because they live life in the moment. They're not afraid to push boundaries and go into uncharted territory. They're into expanding their horizons, and – as I mentioned before – this group inhales the deepest essence of life by truly living in the moment through risk and going to the edge.

Speaking of living in the moment and going to the edge, I have another story for you. It's about the first boy I ever trained. His name was Mike. The first thing I remember about him was his size. I always envisioned Daddies being bigger in stature than their boy counterparts, but I had to throw that idea right out the window when it came to Mike. He was a whopping six foot plus kind of guy and well-built to boot. I'm only five foot five, so he towered over me. The other point that jumps out in my mind was my age.

I was only in my late-20's and just beginning my role as a regional Mr. Drummer as well as a top. I've often heard the cliché that former bottoms make the best tops, but I was so new at giving orders that at times, it felt a little odd. Besides, most people I knew in the lifestyle who were Daddies or Masters were in their late thirties, if not older. I was a pup compared to them, but as the old saying goes, "Everyone has to start somewhere." The night that stands out in my mind was an invite-only dungeon party. I was hanging out with a fellow boy just turned Top/Daddy named Chuck. The two of us were as thick as thieves and always up for mischief. My boy Mike was very nervous but wanted Chuck and I to take him through his first Dungeon experience. Chuck was up for a Daddy tag-team night, and I totally trusted him to follow through in helping me create the ultimate experience for my boy. The stage was set. We arrived at the location and had a little chat with Mike in the parking lot. We told him what to expect when we got inside and went over such formalities as a safety word in case he started to panic or was over-stimulated, etc. We also asked him if he had any special restricted areas he wanted us to avoid. He answered with two things. One restriction was he didn't want anyone in the dungeon touching him except us. The other was he didn't want his jockey shorts (whitie-tighties) taken off in the dungeon because he would feel self-conscious being displayed naked in front of strangers.

Chuck raised an eyebrow in my direction as if to say, "How do we work with that?" I simply smiled and said, "That would be fine." We then proceeded directly inside. I went through the usual registration, waiver and orientation formalities then I went straight for the equipment. I tested everything we intended to use to make sure it worked properly and safely. I had a quick conversation with the Dungeon Master regarding Mike's first restriction. By the time I had finished, Mike and Chuck entered the Dungeon arena. The first thing we did was blindfold him with the bandana I had in my back pocket. The crowd, "in his mind" had vanished and much of his inhibitions with it. Now his world was transformed into one of touch, sound, smell, and taste. Chuck and I quickly dominated him with a hot and sensual rape scene. We took turns holding him down while pulling the clothes from his body, all the while forcing hot passionate kisses into his eager mouth. Chuck and I agreed to remain silent for the better part of the scene and communicated strictly by way of snapping our fingers to signal a switch in position. Mike quickly went off into a world of ecstasy. Chuck and I decisively carried him all through his dungeon journey. One of the high points of the evening for Mike was when we had him in the sling. I easily worked my hands into his briefs and gave him the ride of his life while Chuck worked his nipples and passionately kissed him. Talk about a wet pair of whitie-tighties! Mike got to experience many other things that night from a St. Andrew's cross, being tossed into a cage and fed through the bars, suspension, and even some water sports. So you see, we found a way to work around Mike's rule number two and give him a fulfilling experience just the same.

At the end of the evening the three of us were on a high. Chuck and I gave Mike a hug and sent him home. The two of us went back to my place and cuddled until we fell asleep. Mike later admitted that his experience would have been complete if he'd been invited back to my place with Chuck and tucked in-between us for the night. Once I heard that comment, my lack of experience had given me a big "whack" on the side of the head! After-care, how could I have been so careless!? We took Mike to the top and left him up there. 'One must always bring one's bottom/submissive fully down before sending them off'. I swore never to make that mistake again and I'm happy to say I've stuck to it. The point here is: Mentors are not perfect, and we all have to start somewhere. We get better as we go, so be patient with us. With that in mind don't be afraid to have a spirit for risk and adventure, and you'll experience some wonderful things in your journey!

Another group that always impresses me would have to be those who've had a near-death experience. These individuals have been forced to look Death straight in the eye and are still alive to share the remainder of their life as a changed person. If you've met or known anyone who's had this happen to them, you know what I'm talking about. They have a real grasp of what's important and what really isn't. They have a calm manner and an inner peace in most cases. After all, they should be dead but are still around. Then they're faced with that nagging question of "Why am I still here?" This question leads to many others in a path regarding what one's life-quest, or purpose, is. They make great Mentors and Guides, because they value the time they have left due to their second chance. They also appreciate the little things in life and don't hesitate to stop and smell the roses along the way when the opportunity comes up.

Strangely enough, I've had five near-death experiences, and I can't say any of them were very pleasant. Just the same, I can say I'm definitely a changed person. I have to admit, I wish it only took one experience to do it. I guess I was a bit more resistant to change than I thought. However, the point here is that these individuals will focus on what's important and won't want to waste any time on superficial stuff unless it's in light of having fun. I would rather not share a near-death experience with you because they're usually pretty intense and drawn out. I'd rather share a story of how a Mentor can learn to keep things light and fun while still keeping a serious tone when meeting a new trainee.

This story begins at the gym when I caught Raphe cruising me in the shower one afternoon. He and I were alone, and I was shaving the hair from my shoulders with a razor. Raphe noticed that I couldn't reach a spot along the back side and offered to do it for me. He ended the request with the word "Sir", so I let him do it. While he carefully fulfilled his duty, I noticed his balls had been shaved. I raised one eyebrow and thought, 'Obviously this kid has some experience with a razor.' When he finished he stood at attention and presented me with the razor. I flatly said, "Thank you, I'm going to the steam room to shave my balls." I turned off the water and walked away without a second look. As I opened the door to the steam room, I glanced over my shoulder and noticed that Raphe was fast on my heels. I walked into the steam room to find it was empty.

This was very unusual.

Raphe walked in behind me and I handed him the razor, placed my hands behind my head, and instructed him to "Shave Daddy's balls." He went to his knees and began. After two passes of the razor I was as hard as a rock. He finished the job and, before getting up, gently kissed the head of my hard cock. He then stood at attention and presented the razor. I thought, 'Son of a bitch, what a tease!' So I said "Now it's Daddy's turn to shave yours."

After two passes he was rock hard as well. However, I stopped the play right there saying, "We can get kicked out of here for shit like this. If you want to learn and do more, then meet me in the parking lot, I'll give you my number."

We met and I gave him my number. He was very interested in being collared even though he had no experience in the BD/SM lifestyle. As a matter of fact, he wasn't fully out of the closet. At the time he was living with a girl, but he assured me she was just a roommate. I usually don't start with someone who's not fully out, but there was something about him that reminded me of my younger self so I took him under my wing.

The next group intrigued me. They're the intellectuals and people of action, the free-thinkers and book readers, those who specialize in philosophy, psychology, science, and the arts.

As I mentioned before, as much as I think it's a perfect and peaceful world, I'm also realistic. There are people out there that know that the ignorant and uneducated can easily be manipulated and prefer that you stay that way. So educate yourself or at least surround yourself with highly educated people. They're less likely to be fooled by the illusions of the corrupt portions of society and individuals that perpetuate it.

I like to think of them as the sentinels on the watch towers of life, free expression, and diversity. They keep their eyes on the horizon and nothing much misses their ever-present gaze. There is great value in wisdom and education. This type of Mentor will challenge your intellect and get you thinking from different points of view. Acceptance of the norm is usually not an option; always asking questions is their motto. What better Mentor or Guide to have than someone who stimulates the way you think?

This reminds me of another story. This story is about my friend and confidant Alex C, who came from the great city of New York. Alex moved from New York to Phoenix when I came to be her friend. Now this was a woman of great intelligence, depth, and, I must admit, BD/SM skill. She used to tell me stories of New York and how she'd been trained by the Old Guard. She also shared the fact that she trained boys back there. I found the idea of a female training boys very interesting. She did admit that in Phoenix the boys had a tendency to follow their dicks before their heads and, therefore, didn't approach her for training like they did back east. This surprised me, and so I often shared my view; if a Mentor doesn't fit the mainstream profile, it doesn't mean you should disregard them. There are many great Mentors out there. Often times you can learn a great deal by going outside the lines so to speak. Granted, that person may not make your dick hard but if you acknowledge that going into the situation then a lot of good can come from it. To prove the point, I met with one of my boys and asked his opinion regarding a scene with Alex and myself. He agreed. We ended up having a great time together, and it opened up some new horizons for all of us. Now Alex often refers to him as her boy, and he gladly accepts the title. Phoenix has really grown up over the years, and I'm glad I was around to witness it. Since then, I've seen all sorts of interesting and diverse relationships that revolve around Mentorship and training rather than sex.

Just thought I'd provide a little food for thought in case the situation presents itself.

Speaking of going outside the lines, I'd like to share the story about my two Daddies, Joe and Roger. They're not Leathermen but are 100% Daddies just the same. I think back, I believe they were looking for more of a pool boy but ended up with me instead. The combination couldn't have worked out better. I added a lot of spice and diverse entertainment to their lives, and they kept me out of a lot of trouble that I wasn't mature enough to handle. I was an impetuous youth to say the least, but Joe and Roger didn't give up on me. They practically had to sit on me to keep me in line, but somehow they managed. Not to mention my wild, kinky, BD/SM Fetish side. It's funny, but at the time I was often asked by the local Leather community why I called Joe and Roger my Daddies, even though they weren't into the BD/SM Fetish scene. I would simply reply, "Because that's what they are."

It was then that I learned that you don't have to be into the "Leather lifestyle" to be a Mentor or a Daddy. Joe and Roger had many of the key Daddy qualities of a great Mentor and Guide. They accepted me for who I was, and encouraged me to explore my interests in fetish, even though it wasn't their particular cup of tea. They were very honest and shot from the hip. I may not like what they had to say some of the time, but at least I knew where they stood. They would offer advice but knew I had to make my own mistakes and often stepped back so I could fall on my face. However, they were always there to brush me off and send me on my way again. To this day I can always count on them for encouragement or advice. When it's all said and done I will always call them my two Daddies. So you see, even a Daddy needs his Daddies.

The last group I'd like to touch upon would be those with military and/or a martial arts background. I like to think of them as "the highly disciplined." The Mentors or Guides with martial arts training and those with a military background have some striking similarities. They both have endured a variety of both mental and physical tests, and have a deep-seeded respect for rank and order. Trust is earned and not given lightly. The training in many cases revolves around the balance between life, death, and pain. Because of this, many deep bonds are forged between members of the same unit or Dojo. In combat, they conquer their fears both with others and while alone. It's no wonder these experiences carry over so easily to a Mentor's training style.

Guy Baldwin refers to the former military in his book "The Ties That Bind" when he discusses the Old Guard and their history. He also does a great job describing how it impacted many of the Leathermen and how their rituals and traditions came to be. He discusses how social conditions changed the way they passed down these traditions from Daddy to boy over the years. I suggest checking it out for a better understanding of these concepts. This reminds me of how martial arts changed my experience in the BD/SM world.

As I mentioned earlier, I took up martial arts as a matter of protection and survival when I first entered the BD/SM lifestyle, but ended up getting something much different from it than originally intended. What did I get? Well, humility came first. I got beat up a lot. They used to throw me in the ring with all the black-belts as target practice. I used to come home with black-and-blues all over my butt. My two Daddies would see them when I got out of the shower and comment.

"What the hell are they doing to you at that Dojo?" I would say "I got off easy, they were just humiliating me. They could easily have broken my arm or cracked my ribs for lowering my guard but instead just left black and blues on my ass." However, as my skill increased and ranking climbed humility gave way to respect and then a deep sense of comradery.

There was a strong sense of loyalty to my Dojo and the fellow members of my unit/club. I know it may sound odd, but through all the pain, suffering, and hardship we bonded.

My next step was attaining complete focus and the ability to block out everything: to fully immerse myself in the art form in order to perform it flawlessly. This led to meditation and a high level of inner peace. So, looking back on it all, you could say I got what I originally intended and something much, much more. No wonder a Mentor or Guide would find himself falling back on these life experiences when creating a bonding experience with his mentee.

Mentors and Guides with a military or martial arts background usually have a deep sense of order, respect, and discipline. They often display good manners and humility when appropriate. What better example to pass on to a mentee?

I'd like to share a little story with you about a Daddy with just such a background and how he changed my way of thinking when it came to being a submissive.

This story takes place in Albuquerque, NM. The Daddy's name was Walter. He was a fascinating man. Walter was a well-respected juvenile probation officer and also an established martial artist. Being a high ranking black belt, he went around the country qualifying new black-belts when he wasn't working cases in his home state. Walter was highly educated and had a quiet charisma that was comforting to be around.

On this particular occasion, I was visiting Rico (Walter's boy) and attending one of Albuquerque's local Leather contests.

I was invited to stay at Walter's house and go to the contest with the two of them. It just so happened that Walter was somewhat of a Leather icon in the community at the time, and was asked to be a judge. The night of the contest, Rico came up to me and asked if I would join him in collar and leash at Walter's side. This idea did not go over very well with me at all. I did have a great deal of respect for Walter because of our mutual bond through martial arts, but I also had a very strong GDI streak left in me and had big issues with giving up my personal power and freedom. The idea of being led around on a leash smacked of being demoralized in a way I wasn't willing to do for anyone. Rico tried to convince me of how much fun it would be to no avail. I wasn't going to budge on this one.

Then Walter came over and had a little chat with me. He asked me my concerns regarding the matter and why it bothered me so much. I simply told him I didn't like the idea of being led around like a dog and being passed around like a meaningless piece of property.

It was degrading

Walter let out a sigh of understanding and then explained a few things. First he said, "You will not be treated as anything less. As a matter of fact, you will be treated as something somewhat more." This got my interest, so I was willing to listen to his sales pitch, even though I was still very skeptical. He then went on to explain that he would be more like my bodyguard or protector rather than my owner. What seemed like degrading customs were actually safeguards to protect me.

"Like what?" I asked.

"Well," he said, "no one would be able to address you directly without going through me first. That way I could weed out all of the riff-raff and clingy trolls so you wouldn't have to deal with them. After all, this is my territory and I know everyone in it." Walter went on to mention a few other points in order to put my mind more at ease. After everything was said I reluctantly decided to give it a try.

When we arrived at the contest, Rico advised me to walk behind Walter at all times unless instructed. I shot him a look like "You've got to be kidding!" but played along with it as we entered the front door. Walter was then greeted by many hot Leathermen. All of which patiently waited to be introduced to us by Walter. I kind of liked having Walter as a block and tackle, so I quickly began to relax into the part. Then, Walter sat down at one of the bar stools. Rico gestured for the two of us to sit by his feet, under the bar! Rico assumed the position and motioned for me to do the same. I rolled my eyes and followed his lead. Once I was down there everything changed. This was a much different world than the one above... First of all the view was much better. I was now face to face with Walter's crotch with easy access to it. Not to mention his hot leather pants and boots. I also like the fact that there was no smoke to bother my eyes. Then Rico tapped my shoulder and pointed down the length of the bar. I broke into the biggest Cheshire smile as I saw a sea of hot crotches, Leatherwear and boots. Then this big bear paw of a hand reached down and lightly rubbed my stubble covered jaw. The scent and feel of Walter's leather gloves on my face was intoxicating. A moment later a drink was handed down to me. At that moment I thought 'Now this is heaven' and I have to admit, my view of the situation had dramatically changed. I also have to confess I did indulge myself with Walter's crotch while under the bar that night and it made for a very hot fantasy. The contest followed and the rest, as I like to say, is history. Thinking back, I do miss Walter and often wonder where life has placed him. He did however introduce me to another man from Albuquerque named Pat Sanchez who became a dear friend and Mentor. Pat walked me through a few more steps in my understanding of things, but that my friends is another story.

Well, I think that's enough story telling for now, and I've covered all the life experience categories I set out to explore. I just want to share a few more thoughts regarding them:

Mentors and Guides come in all different shapes, sizes, walks of life, genders, fetishes, and personalities. Everyone is a Mentor or Guide, but not everyone knows it most of the time. The difference is some have chosen to make this a primary focus in their lives. They do this in many ways. They try to live a life based on simple core principles.

They realize they're a work in the making and acknowledge that they're not perfect. They make mistakes like everyone else but can easily laugh at themselves and see the humor in it.

There are all different levels of Mentors and Guides. Some have taken the time to master more of the core principles than others but all are on the same path. They're often givers and take joy in bringing happiness to others' lives. You often find them contributing some of their time or money to one charitable organization or another. Even though they may not say so, they have an inner desire to try and make the world a better place while they're around.

They don't need to be on a stage speaking to thousands even though some do. Some conduct workshops or put together presentations as well as write books. Many are aware of the Butterfly- or Ripple- Effect and how one changed life can affect thousands so they prefer to remain out of the spotlight and work in a more intimate "one-on-one" setting. Whatever the path the Mentor or Guide has chosen, it always leads toward personal growth, inner-peace, and happiness.

I'm not saying life with a Mentor or Guide is peaceful, stress-free, and always harmonious. On the contrary, it can be just the opposite. This is someone who's going to bust you on all your bullshit and expect the same in return. This is a time for "no masks" and getting around to all of your basic truths no matter how ugly they may seem. Remember, it's all about trust, acceptance, and unconditional love. You need to have a good foundation, and the Mentor or Guide knows that with or without sex, a good foundation is mandatory, so be prepared to be challenged.

They're always reminded that a Mentor is a guide as well as teacher, and Guides make discoveries as they travel along this path as well. They look at themselves as Way showers in uncharted waters for the young and inexperienced. They're also daring adventurers who challenge boundaries for those more experienced. The biggest difference you'll find in a Mentor or Guide is they will not try to change someone into what "they" think they should be. The Mentor would rather support and offer guidance knowing that everyone must follow their own path. They know there must be rules regarding honesty and trust but will leave the boy/mentee's self-expression and individuality intact.

1020

The beauty in every person is the full expression of themselves as they truly are without feeling stifled or repressed.

By the way, this doesn't mean the boy can run amok and do whatever he pleases. It just means he has the freedom to become what he was meant to be.

Here's a great analogy I would like to share with you that might help make things easier to understand. Think of the boy or mentee as a beautiful painting. This painting is not yet finished and still needs a frame. The Mentor looks at the painting and says, "What a beautiful painting." The Mentor doesn't try and make the painting fit into a frame that doesn't fit just because he's more comfortable or likes it. He also doesn't pick a frame that overpowers the painting, lest it be overwhelmed and loses its beauty. Rather, the Mentor or Guide will ask, "What kind of frame would I put on this to best complement and support it?" The Mentor then becomes the frame which supports the painting. As the painting grows and changes so does the frame which supports it. Both complement each other and the full beauty of the painting can be revealed.

So, I guess we've gone full circle on this, and I've covered a lot of ground, but where does it leave you? Hopefully it leads you to more questions. It's only by asking questions that we truly grow, but what really matters is the type of questions you ask yourself as a Mentor, Guide, or person looking for one.

A good one to start with is: "What do I want?" Most people would like a Mentor or Guide but haven't thought about what it is they want the Mentor to guide them through. That's the first thing I find out about any potential mentee. It would be nice if they already knew the answer, but it's not necessary. Any Mentor or Guide knows it's a journey you take together and all the discoveries will come in their own good time. As I've mentioned before, "It's not what you show up with but rather what you leave with that matters."

Chapter 4: Being Responsible

Being Responsible and having
Purpose in Today's World

This chapter runs hand in hand with the last one. Being responsible in today's world means many things, so I decided to write a chapter regarding some of these views, because even though they do hold the same basic truths, the subject matter is different.

Being responsible takes many forms and applies to many areas of our lives. I've observed others who displayed high levels of personal responsibility in the attempt to try and understand what motivates them. I've searched within myself for answers.

I've read books on the subject and made some discoveries. I believe I've come to an understanding why so many do and do not want to be responsible in today's world. The answer once again is a simple one: "Which is easier?" Many times it's not the easy choice but the right one that makes the difference between being responsible, having integrity, and staying true than doing what's convenient.

I'm going to share some life stories with you that will shed some light on some of the areas of this multifaceted concept.

Let's start out with my early days in the Leather community and being a young title holder. I remember losing a number of contests back in those days because I was self-centered and thought holding a community Leather title was like being a Leather Mr. Universe. You just showed up at events to look sexy on stage then went on with your life as soon as you stepped off the stage. I'd often get pissed off when I didn't win the contest and wondered what I was doing wrong. It didn't take long to realize that a title in any form was a pledge of service to your community and a sponsor. Once that sunk in, I became part of the community and started to earn titles. This reminds me of a conversation with a former title holder named Dan Leg.

The story starts out the day after he passed his title to me.

He sat me down for a little talk and basically ripped me a new one. He lectured me about how I should run my title. He said he didn't want to see the title he worked so hard on over the past year be handed over to someone who was going to sit on their ass.

He wanted to make sure I was going to follow through with it and be fully involved in the community. He wanted to see me doing a number of charity events throughout the year as well as other community support events. I was taken aback by all this at first because I already had plans in the works for all these things.

Then I realized I was seeing Dan's love for the community and didn't take it personally. Recently there had been a number of contestants who won titles then dropped the ball or just moved away without notice. This was just his personal way of sending off the next ship with a clear conscience. I gave him my word and stuck to it. However, it came at a price. I worked hard all that year doing everything I promised. Then, just before International Mr. Leather (IML), I got the job of a lifetime and was forced to stay in Phoenix to complete new-hire training. I sent my first runner-up in my place. He said it was a great experience, and I was happy to give him the opportunity, even though it was something I always wanted. For a while I often wondered what it would have been like and what friends I would have made.

Oh well, you can't change the past. Besides, I already got the real payoff. I found the rewards of becoming a bigger part of my community. The friendships and memories I made that year were worth their weight in gold. Besides, I thought if I wanted to continue my pursuit in community service, there's always other titles I could run for. Then again, who needs a title to be involved in the community anyway? If you want to, just do it!

One thing did get my attention. It was strange to see, but I noticed the number of contestants for these contests drop dramatically at the beginning of the new millennium. Local contest would only have one "Mister" contestant and maybe two boys competing. Back in the 80's and early-90's you would see at least five or more in each category. I wondered why, so I started asking questions in the hope of finding some answers. When I asked the youth of the upcoming generations why they weren't competing for a title they said they weren't interested. I asked, "Why?" After all, I could see they were very interested in the play and social aspects of the BD/SM Fetish community.

The answers I got back were as follows...:

"I don't have the time."

"What do they need me for?"

"Can't someone else do it?"

"I'm just not interested right now."

"I have too much going on in my personal life and just want to take care of me."

"What's in it for me?"

"No way, Man; that's too much work."

Over all it seemed the majority of them had more concern for themselves and their immediate friendships rather than the community at large. I was surprised and asked myself how this could have happened. As I looked back into my past, I once again believe I found one of the reasons for this shift in thinking.

Back when there was the overwhelming threat of death and hardship during the AIDS outbreak, people had a reason to band together. They felt they had something meaningful to fight for. It gave them a purpose. Titles and community service were the vehicle in which money was raised to help save lives. Now that the immediate threat seems to have vanished or lost its intensity so the desire for such positions became less desirable.

Some realities are sad even though they are true. However let's not forget the key point here: "Having a sense of purpose." Maybe all that's lacking is a shift of perspectives from one type of purpose to another. If someone doesn't have a sense of purpose for something greater than themselves, then of course they're going to revert back to self-preservation, personal interests, and immediate friendships. There's no desire to strive for anything better than themselves. This is where inspiration comes into play. When we inspire someone, we present them with a new way of thinking. We give them a purpose that's bigger than themselves, and they find that the rewards of such a life are much more fulfilling than the one they had. They are empowered, and empowered people make great things happen. Anyone can do this. One person can change the world. All you have to do is have a purpose and care deeply enough about it. Just look around and you'll see hundreds of examples of how one person made a big difference. Mahatma Gandhi and Mother Teresa are just two examples. As a matter of fact, Mother Teresa once said, "There's no such thing as great deeds...only small deeds done with great love." So don't count yourself out as being meaningless and insignificant. Everyone has an impact on things. You just have to make a commitment to doing something about it. It's not hard and you don't have to feel like you're dedicating your whole life to a cause. Start small, for instance "your own personal circle of influence" and "as you grow, so will your acts of kindness." Then your perceptions of how to make things better in more creative ways will come to blossom.

How does this relate to the Mentor and his mentee? Well, let's focus on the Mentor for a moment. The task of the up and coming Mentor or Guide is to inspire their mentee in a direction that is purposeful. Not an easy task for a mentee who is so full of life and energy. The main focus is usually on play and experiencing new and exciting things. However the answer is right under your nose. You lead by example. The

Mentor or Guide attends the charity functions and social and cultural events.

He or she just needs to include the mentee as part of his or her life and they'll be exposed to it. The meaning of these events and how they affect the mentee/trainee is not always evident at first, but believe me; everything you do has a part to play in molding the person's perceptions of the world and how they choose to interact with it in the future. Remember, you're in their life to be a Guide not to try and make them anything. It is always a wish of the Mentor that the mentee/trainee become a complete, loving and giving person, but ultimately the true goal is to support them in becoming the full expression of what they truly are. Nothing more.

All mentees are giving people. They start by giving up some control to a Mentor in order to be guided. How deep the level of giving will go depends on the individual, what purpose they are drawn to and how inspired they become.

Over the years I remember all the different functions I've attended and things I've done to do my part giving to this world and being responsible. I'd like to share a few in the hope of bringing some understanding into the picture for those who haven't experienced it.

The first story which comes to mind is the Universal Brotherhood of Leatherlords' Toy Drive.

Once a year, the UBL has a holiday toy drive. The recipient is Logan's Playground (www.logansplayground.org), which is for children or families affected by AIDS. We spend the better part of three months preparing and executing the toy drives. It's a lot of work, and we always try and make it fun for all of the volunteers. We have parties for the kick off, box decorating, pick-up, delivery, and then there's the close out or wrap up. All the volunteers do this in their free time. I'd like to say that everything is peaceful and a state of bliss but it always has its tense moments.

Sometimes I get lost in all the work or in keeping the peace between the brothers and volunteers. I ask myself what all the work is for. Then I tell myself, "The children remember." But even with that, sometimes the feeling wasn't fully felt. However one particular year something changed. I found something I had lost.

I was invited to go down and visit the center the day the toys were being given out. I got the information mixed up and thought it was another wrap up party so I brought a friend to sit and enjoy some coffee and mingle. When we arrived we were very warmly greeted. We were quickly introduced to all of the volunteer staff as they busily ran about bringing out toys for the line of families waiting to sit on Santa's lap and make a wish. As we waited to say hello to one of main organizers, I noticed a very large box just in front of Santa which was filled with small stuffed animals for each child before sitting on Santa's lap. I looked down to see a little girl in a white jacket holding her mother's hand. She had deep brown eyes and beautiful brown hair. However the box towered over her and she had no idea what was inside. I smiled and told her mom about the stuffed animals. She quickly found something her daughter would like and handed it to her. The little girls eyes lit up and the most beautiful smile came across her face. My eyes traveled from that little girl all the way up the line of children and it finally sunk in. Sometimes you need to see the lives you're affecting to keep the feeling alive. After long periods of staying on the operational side of things you have a tendency to forget.

I experienced this feeling much more often when I did Meals-on-Wheels, because I was so closely involved with the people I delivered to. I saw a movie called "Latter Days" (2003), which paints a good picture of what I was like when I started delivering Meals-on-Wheels. If you want a good visual, then I recommend seeing it. However the point is, you don't need to pick something HIV related. Everyone is inspired by different things. Find the thing you feel passionate about and do something about it. So what are you waiting for? It's never too late to do something.

Taking action is a crucial part of being responsible. Anyone can say "Yeah, I'm responsible," but ask them to show you how and you may get a different answer.

Being responsible takes many forms. This reminds me of another story that happened at the local Leather bar. One of my Brothers came to me one day very upset. I asked him what was bothering him so he told me. He and another of my Leather Brothers were working at the local Leather bar during the slow period. On the other side of the bar was what they called a self-proclaimed Top and Master. They knew of him and the fact that he had little to no experience but boasted that he did at every opportunity. They usually tried to ignore him as they served him drinks but on this particular day they lost it.

It seems he was bragging about the new slave he picked up on the Internet. The slave was moving from his home state to live with this Top. He was saying all the things he was going to do to him. After all, he was the Master and the slave was obliged to do whatever he commanded without question. One of the top things on this Master's list was to have sex with the slave without protection and deliberately infect him with HIV. As the Master put it, "I'm going to fuck that slave and breed his hole positive!" Well, that's all it took. My Brothers lost it. They said they leaned into the guy with everything they had. I guess they "ripped him a new one," so to speak.

I have to admit it's a tough line to walk because there are those who would actually support the Master by stating two important BD/SM rules. One, was the act consensual? Two, the Master, unlike a Daddy/boy relationship, does have final say on whatever he wishes to do to his slave. Makes you think doesn't it.

My thoughts on this are "What is the morally correct thing to do?" I've had many boys who were negative ask me to play unsafely with them and climax in them. They said they wanted to feel the passion of the moment. After all, the medical community is now getting away from using the term AIDS and moving towards HIV because it's becoming a more manageable condition. I said no and explained that it was a personal decision and it would be wrong to infect another person even if they didn't care. It was something I didn't want to live with. After all, the BD/SM rules we follow so sacredly also state, "Safe and Sane." There are all different levels of safe and sane behavior. Some things are by nature more risky than others.

Now comes the big one: What about unprotected sex between two people who are already HIV positive? Boy, this one has caused more debate and headaches than I can imagine. I remember it being a bear trap question the judges used to use at leather contests. On one hand the contestant wanted to preach Safe, Sane and Consensual sex but also didn't want to be dishonest because they didn't actively practice safe sex all the time with other positive players. What a dilemma: how to avoid looking like a hypocrite even though what they do in their own personal time is their own affair. It was a tough call at best. The way that I look at it is this.

If someone is out there doing their best to try and educate and promote prevention, then it's better not to try and judge their personal life. Would you want them judging yours? In the end they have to live with the choices they make just like you do.

However, the topic of two HIV positive people having unsafe sex is one of the main reasons some of the young people today want to become infected. The medical field strongly suggests against this because of concerns of breeding a stronger, more resistant strain of virus. Others say there is no substantial proof of this or just don't care. Someone newly infected, or as I've heard it referred to as Newly Converted, often think "Now it's done and I can just bare-back with anyone that's positive"; "There are plenty of hot guys out there who I can really let go and get it on with."

Think again my friends, suddenly insurance coverage and co-pays for medication become an important part of your life. It also becomes a permanent part of your life. Sure condoms aren't as fun as full contact but that doesn't negate their importance.

There's also one other point to consider. I went to a Man to Man retreat a while back. It pointed out another perspective. The facilitator said that someone's body who's already HIV positive is already dealing with one virus. Why risk unsafe sex and picking up another STD for your body to fight? Then along with HIV you end up with Herpes, Hepatitis C, etc.

So you see the debate goes on ad nauseam.

An RN friend of mine named DJ once described it to me like this: "Blade," he said, "if you go to that corner of the room and I go to the opposite corner of the room and we jack off, we'll be having totally safe sex. Anything more will require some level of risk. So no matter what kind of play you are engaging in, there is some level of risk. It's up to you to decide how far you want to go and be willing to accept the consequences for your actions.

"After all, we can't live like we're in plastic separation body suits all our lives."

The bottom line is that it's your body; do as you see fit. Just remember how it affects others not just your own before you do anything.

Personally speaking, take it from someone who's positive.

There are different activities that are available to enjoy that lead up to sex. Take care of yourself, your body, and your partner. If you still want more answers about sexual intimacy, then the next two chapters will be very helpful.

In wrapping up, you can see there are many different facets to being responsible. Only you can decide which makes sense and works in a way in which you can live with yourself and the choices you make. All I can add is with a sense of purpose, being responsible is more fulfilling and enjoyable. All you need to do is decide what path you want to take.

Chapter 5: The Journey

"The road we travel together."

"There are many roads in life, but this road we travel together." I can't think of a better statement to sum up the relationship of a Mentor and his mentee than this. Well, if you want to set out on any road in life, you're going to need a road map and, if you're lucky, a Guide. As with anything else, maps offer direction and will keep you out of harm's way. With that in mind, let's get started. Just remember that every person's life experience is different; therefore, their road map will be just as unique.

Road maps change as you go, so don't think you're going to stay with the same one all your life. Be prepared to make adjustments. A good case in point is the idea I had that I was always going to stay a boy. After all, once I got comfortable with the role, I really loved it. Life had other plans in store for me, however. And even though I was a bit uncomfortable with the Top/Sir role at first, I wouldn't change my current role as a Mentor and Guide for anything. I love being a Daddy!

Where do you start? Once again, the answer is "What do you want?" Make sure you're clear about what you want. By this, I mean if you're looking for someone who's supposed to fix or do everything for you, then think back about the Baby Huey story I shared earlier. You attract what you are. So if you're in it strictly for self-serving motives, then you may want to think about this a bit more before continuing. After all, if you want to attract someone who's self-reliant and strong, then you'll want to be self-reliant and strong yourself. That person will be attracted to someone with the same potential.

Second, ask yourself what you want to explore sexually.

Believe me; the emotional stuff will take care of itself. Many times I've had long talks over dinner or coffee regarding what a potential boy wants sexually and what his concerns are.

Many times I've heard them say they had trust issues and the inability to let go of control. Remember: trust is earned, so be clear about what you want so the Mentor or Guide can be trusted not to cross any boundaries that weren't brought to his attention. It takes time to rebuild trust so you don't want to start off on a bad note even if it is an accident. Don't get overly concerned with emotions; as trust grows, all the emotions come pouring out. It's a natural progression.

Many people show up with no idea where to start. There's nothing wrong with that. It's great to have a spirit for adventure.

I like to offer the old tried and true hanky code list. It's a great introduction to one of the Old Guard traditions and sparks the imagination of the reader. I've often had a new mentee highlight the hanky colors that interest him as well as what pocket he would like to wear them in. I follow up with my choices off the list and then check off the ones we have in common. We start with these. It doesn't take long before we're venturing outside their original choices. So, you see the first steps on this new road can be just that easy. Nowadays, there's a color for anything and the "hanky lists and color codes" can easily be found on the Internet. What a great world we live in!

Flagging a hanky is a great conversation starter and it also let's interested parties know what you're in the mood for. I can't count how many times guys have come up to me and asked me what my hanky color means and why I wear it in the left pocket. Let's just say it's led to some very colorful conversations.

Now let's get back to the journey. This is a journey of giving.

Remember I mentioned earlier that it's all about the boy. Well, I think now would be a good time to elaborate on this. New and up-coming Daddies take heed, because this is for you.

The first thing to remember is: "You can never give too much as long as you're giving willingly." Make no mistake, if one or the other of you feels taken advantage of or you're resentful for giving, then it's not authentic and it loses its strength. This comes into play most significantly when the phrase, "It's all about the boy," enters the scene. One of the greatest epiphanies I've had was putting the boy first and knowing I would still be fully in control and sexually satisfied at the same time. Putting the boy or mentee first and catering to their fantasy or needs doesn't leave the Top or Daddy out in the cold. On the contrary, what happens is the boy pulls you into his fantasy and the two of you go on the trip together. Believe me when I tell you you're not going to be left out in the cold. For instance, I've had boys tell me that they only climax once and they're done for the evening. I would simply reply, "With time, I could get you to five times. You've just trained your body over time to accept one as enough." This reminds me of Matt. He had a wonderful tattoo covering his back with the word SLAVE. He was faced with this very same challenge. Over the course of reaching his five climax goal, we used to engage in a series of scenes searching each other's bodies to find every trigger to achieve a climax. Back and forth we'd go, over and over again. A couple weeks after we started Matt was at climax number four and fell over onto the bed. I asked him how he felt, and he replied, "I'm completely exhausted and exhilarated at the same time!" His next question really got me though. He said, "You only came three times so far; do you want me to get you off now?" Did I feel left out? I think not.

Balloon Boy Brett was another prime example of this concept of the "It's-all-about-the-boy" mind set. When I first started Mentoring Brett I didn't have a lot of experience with balloon play. Come to find out, neither did Brett but he did know what turned him on and wanted a lot of it. So I used my best imagination and went right to work building fantasies around balloons. Brett got so turned on by what I came up with. I, in turn, got turned on by his sexual energy. He pulled me right into his fantasy world. We had many wonderful scenes together. I never thought I would fully enjoy balloon play, but Brett opened my mind and heart to his world. One of my favorite scenes didn't even revolve around balloon play even though it had a little in it. However, this story was all about the boy so I'll share it with you.

I always liked to keep my boys guessing on what I have in store for them. On this occasion I set out a hat on the coffee table at Brett's place. Then I instructed him to take three blank pieces of paper and write down three fantasies he would like to explore that day. I informed him I would be doing the same.

Then we folded them, placed them in the hat and stirred them up. Then I instructed Brett to pick out three of the six. We would make these three the scene for the day. The first one chosen was his. It said, "Tie up Daddy." The next two were mine. They said, "A room with a view," and the last, "A room without a view." As you can see, I always like to keep my boys guessing. The answer to the puzzle of the room with a paradox view was easily revealed once we arrived at the local bathhouse. This location had two dungeon rooms with slings and we got the one with the sling over the bed. I had Brett in his collar and he was very formal in his actions. We dropped our duffel bags in the room and got started settling in.

This was a new experience for Brett, but I could tell he already liked it. Now he understood the meaning of the paradox regarding the room's view. The room had no windows, so there was no view. However, just by leaving the door open you had a very good view of all the hot men strolling by the room in just towels. But fair is fair and we had the first request from the hat to fulfill. With that in mind I shut the door and climbed naked into the sling. Brett blindfolded me and tied me to the chains of the sling. He then blew up a balloon and balanced it in the cleft of my chest. In nothing but his collar, he began to service my cock and balls with an intensity he'd never done before. That boy had me begging for mercy and the release of my load. When it came it covered the balloon hovering on my chest. Did we stop there? No. We switched places and I returned the favor. After which time, I escorted Brett to the showers where we washed each other down. Then a funny thing happened. While Brett was busy servicing my back with his soapy hands, I noticed a very handsome fellow staring at the two of us. He had a thick red goatee and a short almost military-style haircut. I also couldn't help but notice the very large bulge coming from his towel. I smiled and nodded and he returned the nod with a smile. I guess it was a nice scene watching a boy in collar soap up his Daddy's back.

Even though the thought of going a round with him was very tempting I knew it was all about my boy and the initial scene had been completed. With that in mind I redirected my attention back to Brett. After we showered, we made our way back to the room and were greeted with a pleasant surprise. Standing in the hallway outside our room was none other than Mr. Bulge. I thought, 'What the heck,' I called my boy over and asked him if he'd like to go another round with the Daddy in the hall. Much to my surprise Brett said, "Yes," with a big grin. This time we tag teamed Mr. Bulge. We popped him into the sling and off went the towel. The two of us hardly gave him a moment to come up for air. Brett went for the grand prize between his legs and I straddled the sling by standing on the bed and fed Mr. Bulge everything he could handle that was between my furry cheeks.

It didn't take long before I could feel his body convulsing as he surrendered his load. The second scene was even better than the first one! What a great ride. As we said our good-byes to Mr. Bulge, he said he would leave his name and number at the front desk because he liked us and would love to stay in touch.

As we turned in our towels during check out, I asked the front desk if Mr. Bulge had left his contact information. Much to our surprise he had indeed left his information and we found out he was actually the owner of the club! You should have seen Brett's face light up on that one!

Often it's the scene behind the scene, the unexpected or unplanned scene that's the topper. The key is to always be open to these opportunities when they arise, but remember not to become self-centered with your priorities. There's always plenty to go around. Be patient because it all comes back to you three-fold when you play your cards right. Just remember, it's all about the boy.

(As a side note, thank you Brett. You're a ray of light in a weary world and the most playful of all boys I had the pleasure of Mentoring.)

However, just because it's "all about the boy" doesn't mean he always gets his way. This brings me back to Raphe the boy who had a habit of being late. Well, I have another story about Raphe that fits this situation perfectly. It was my second date with Raphe and on this occasion Raphe and I were at one of the local Leather bars on a busy night. Raphe was very nervous, but I assured him I would look out for him and make sure he would be safe. After all, Raphe wasn't fully out of the closet yet, so this was a huge step.

Once we were in, Raphe stuck close to my side. I had already taught him many of the Old Guard social protocols so he knew how to handle himself fairly well for a newcomer. At one point we were in a conversation with a very experienced bottom named Steve. I had known Steve for many years and since he was between Daddies at the time, he enjoyed our company. I asked Steve to take Raphe over to the bar's leather shop while I went to get drinks for the two of us. I wanted to see how Raphe would do while he wasn't attached to my hip so to speak. When I rejoined them they had questions regarding some of the equipment displayed in the shop. I answered their questions and noticed that Raphe was still puzzled by the cock rings. A scene quickly formed in my head. I whispered into Steve's ear and he responded with a nod and smile. I bought one of the cock rings and then Steve and I took Raphe into the bathroom, the "Tea Room." We pushed him into a stall and wedged the two of us in as well. Steve was instructed to supply Raphe with deep passionate kisses and work his upper body while I stripped open his pants and mounted the new cock ring on his ever hardening cock. Steve and I worked him over and brought him to a climax in what seemed like seconds. It was a momentary flash and then it was over. We all emerged from the bathroom with smiles of victory. Especially Raphe, he was lit up like a Christmas tree! He was visibly shaking and I couldn't get him to stop talking about how hot the whole scene was. Just the same, one thing did make me pause.

Raphe couldn't stop talking about how hot Steve's kissing was. He literally went on about it for five minutes. When he finally settled down he asked me to kiss him. I said "No".

Raphe didn't like that answer and asked why. I brought to his attention the fact that he just spent the last five minutes raving about how well Steve kissed. No matter how hard Raphe tried, he would still unconsciously compare my kissing to Steve's so therefore I wasn't going to do it. Raphe wasn't buying it and still pressed to get his first kiss from me. He tried all night long and came up with every excuse in the book to get his way without success of course. I made Raphe wait a month before I gave him his first kiss. We were in the middle of an entirely different scene, and I laid it on him. It took his breath away.

After the scene was over he looked at me and said, "Now I understand." "Thank you, that was incredible!" So when it comes to being "all about the boy," I guess you can say not getting your way can also be very nice too.

Now we've come full circle with the topic of "It's all about the boy." Just remember, when making life long memories for our boys/mentee's we make them for ourselves. We're all interconnected.

Speaking of interconnectedness, this also brings me to another point in your togetherness. There are times when your alone or apart. Remember, physical proximity is not relationship, the heart and mind are. Letting go can be one of the hardest things a Mentor or his mentee can do. Sometimes you may not feel ready for the physical separation but it may need to happen anyway. This is when as a friend of mine put it, "The moment when Life/the Universe pulls out all the stops to test your capacity for unconditional love." After all, it's easy to let go of something you don't want but very hard to let go of something you love deeply. Even after the active training portion of the relationship has ended or moved on, the interconnectivity of the two individuals remains forever. You've become intertwined in your life experience and therefore you'll always be connected on some level. It's a continuing process.

You're only preparing yourself for the next Mentor/ Guide or next life experience. Feeling separated or alone is just an illusion.

You're never alone, sometimes it just seems that way.

Well, now that you have the beginnings of a road map it's time to enter the dance. I like to use the analogy of a dance because "it takes two to Tango" so to speak. Although the two individuals are separate in their experience they are one in their journey. How remarkable and amazing this special dance is. One chooses to lead and the other to follow. The more experienced partner guides the other through the dance. Both partners are of equal importance and make a conscious effort to do their part in this sensual and erotic dance. If one slips, the other is there to catch and support. Over time the partners become very accustomed to each other's moves so the dance becomes effortless and the two seem as one. Bonds become close and the two share many special experiences together.

The BD/SM, Fetish sexual dance of intimacy is one you'll never forget once you've experienced it. It's one of diversity and exploration. It's an exchange of many things including personal energy, pain, passion and love.

The above statement is rather poetic but if you've ever seen someone wield duel floggers or the motion of a bull whip as it glides through the air when it rounds for the next crack, then you understand what this dance looks like. For the less experienced, there may have been a moment when you've been in an intense sexual encounter and held the other with a fixed gaze, "eye to eye consumed in rapture?" It's as if "for that moment" time stands still. This is the arena the Mentor or Guide seeks to take the counterpart. In this moment time collapses. I recall many occasions when I've emerged from a scene with one of my boys only to find that many hours had passed. I refer to this as being a "Time Bubble." For the two of us, time has slowed down or even seems to have stopped. Momentarily, we were separated from the rest of the world and connected in a different place. It's just like my boy Tiger described it. "Everything gets quiet and goes away.

It's very peaceful." Well, maybe not so quiet, but for the two of us, everything else does go away. I always seek to take my boy and myself to this place for a while and then bring us back. Boundaries are challenged and a fantastic growth is experienced. Above all, amazing levels of inner strength, love and bonding are attained. In this special place we make our greatest discoveries together. We grow stronger as individuals and as a pair. Anyone who's been to this place knows what I'm talking about. Anyone who hasn't is most likely intrigued by what I just said and many will be hungry to know more.

How do you know when you've found the right person who can take you to that special place? Difficult question my friend and the only way to answer it is to follow your heart and your head. If your head says that something doesn't seem right before you begin then there's usually a good reason for it. Don't second guess yourself. Many new comers ask why they just keep attracting the same types of people in their life and get discouraged because things never seem to work out.

Just keep in mind one thing. If you didn't fully learn what you were supposed to in the last round, then you'll need to repeat it to some degree until you've fully worked it out. This is a good time to look inward to see what it is that you're doing to attract such people into your life rather than at what the so-called short comings of everyone else are. Once you have found someone you can build strong trust bonds with then follow your heart, let go and open yourself to explore freely without restraint. You'll find yourself in this "special place" in no time at all. The best part is that you can go back as often as you like once you know your way. Just remember, being lost isn't a bad thing. It takes time to find your way. It's a process we all go through so be patient and trust that it will all work out. It's through giving of ourselves and sharing that we become fully alive. Once you're reached it you'll want to go back again and again.

In this day and age it's much more than just the scene.

It's the whole relationship as you choose to build it. When I say "you choose to build it" I mean it. Each partner you choose to dance with will have their own unique style. Their style melds with yours and a new dynamic is created. This is a combining of two life experiences mingled together. Both of you will evolve into different individuals by the time the relationship has run its full course. You'll both become fuller expressions of what you're truly meant to be once you see through the veil of your fears. Everyone has their own unique set of fears. It will take a little time to figure out what they are before you can work through them. For instance, so many people have a fear of not being accepted because they're not fitting in the sexual norm. Now there's a farce! This whole world is designed with diversity as its main blueprint. Think about it. Right down to the smallest snow flake. So why is it that we can't even accept our own diverse sexual desires as just another aspect of ourselves without question? Now then, let's get back on track about the process of how you choose to build your own experience. "Experience" is the key word here.

Life is a chain of life experiences linked together. The goal of the Mentor/Guide is to create as many special and unique moments/experiences as possible to ensure that the chain is beautiful yet strong. The boy or Mentee is the material from which the chain of experiences is forged.

The key here is to explore every aspect of your inner sexual self. Just remember there are the three Holy Grail rules of "Safe, Sane and Consensual." Guy Baldwin does a very good job of describing exactly what he defines as "Safe, Sane and Consensual" in his book "The Ties that Bind." I suggest you check it out if you have any questions defining them. In the meantime, I'd like to quote a friend of mine who said, "Rules are made to protect not prevent." Keep that in mind when you do your exploring. It will keep you out of harm's way. I'm not throwing water on your fire just making sure you have a good foundation. Just as with dancing, you must have a solid stance and good balance. How can you be in a position to catch your partner if you can't support yourself?

Another thing to keep in mind is to get very familiar with your play equipment. I've had some of the best scenes go to hell in a hand basket because of a lack of proficiency with the equipment being used. The person in question had never used it before or hadn't used it in a very long time. Either way, it's a recipe for disaster. A little extra time taken to re-familiarize yourself with any equipment being used will always ensure a good experience.

Now I've mention a few things in previous chapters and I said I would get back to them and elaborate. Well its time I give you my perspective on something many refer to as "After Care". There is proper education in everything and good reasons for it as well. Would you take someone you care about to a dance, give them the time of their life and then just leave them out on the floor? This is what you're doing if you don't participate in After Care. You need to make sure you follow through. Walk them off the dance floor, take them home and hold them for the night if necessary. Everyone's

"After Care" needs are different so you'll have to take the time to find out what they are. It's very dangerous to take someone through a very physically and/or psychologically demanding scene and just expect them to jump in their car afterwards and drive home on their own. Now-a-days, people do it without a second thought. I know from my personal experience that I've had flash backs recalling all of the hot moments I felt during the evening's scene while driving home in my truck. I would get aroused just reliving those moments and wanting to jack off as soon as I got home. Would you say my attention was fully on my driving? I think not.

As I mentioned, everyone's "After Care needs are different.

Some like to be held, others need to have their own space in order to come down. Whichever the case, it's always important to supply your partner the needed time and attention to allow for a full recovery before sending them out into the world again. People are not light bulbs that can be switched on and off. They need time for recovery. Time to catch their breath once someone has taken it away.

Many people think that all of the magic happens during the scene and all of the bonding happens there. Don't sell yourself short. Another big chunk of the magic happens during "After Care." This is where the phrase "A Thundering Velvet Hand" comes into play. Mentor's and their boys can be incredibly strong, there is no doubt. However, it's when we let ourselves be vulnerable to one another that the bonds become even deeper.

I'll give you an example of what a Mentor would say to his boy as he describes what he had in mind for him.

"I'll hold you down, dominate you and make you scream in ecstasy as you surrender yourself to me. When

I'm done I'll rap my arms around your quivering body, hold you close, and kiss the tears from your eyes" Then I'll whisper in your ear "You are going to be alright, Daddy has you." "I'll hold you until your shaking subsides and your breathing is calm once again." Now I've taken you through a small part of this journey with a road map. In many ways it's like a dance, in others it's like forging a strong chain. Whichever analogy you related to the most, I hope you found something to take with you.

Remember everyone's road map is different so take what you want and move on. If you're still a bit puzzled because you were hoping to get a simple clear cut "Do this, twist that nipple and it will happen like magic" then let me clarify something. You can't take this journey through any book. You have to live it.

You have to experience it through your body and the exchange of your sexual energy. This brings us to the next chapter "The Connection" which I believe is the most important. In the meantime, get out there and start experiencing things!

Chapter 6: The Connection

"The intense exchange of sexual energy"

Often when we're young we are taught that Sex equals Love. This causes an interesting dynamic in some gay BD/SM men. On the one hand they want the meaningfulness of having that beautiful love relationship and then have this opposing need to be a total sex pig without restraint and inflict on their sexual partner things they could never do with someone they love so deeply for fear of hurting them. Now isn't that a bear trap. What to do with two opposing voices in your head. I wouldn't call that a win-win situation. This situation requires a letting go or shift in one's way of thinking in order to find balance. There are a lot of relationships where inflicting pain on a partner is looked at as a true pleasure, bonding experience or release from daily pressures. From this point of view the experience of giving and receiving pain is a gift rather than something that damages the relationship. It's just that simple.

If you're still having a problem wrapping your arms around this concept then please refer to Guy Baldwin's book "The Ties that Bind". He goes into much more detail regarding this matter and it may help.

Now let's get back to this sex equals love dynamic. I know when I was young I was taught that sex and love should be as one because it was the most fulfilling. However, I found out very quickly in the gay world of living in LA that things were much different. I was just another hot young buck who moved into the city from some small Podunk town back east and green as the day was long. Every time I'd sleep with a hot guy I thought it was going to mean love and a relationship but quickly found out I was just a piece of meat to them. I was just another conquest or notch in the bed post. Rather than experience getting my heart stomped on repeatedly I quickly separated sex from love. It just made sense. Men are built as mating machines and think about it all the time. There was no malicious intent here, just a need for sexual release. Once I understood this, tricking was no problem. I would go into a bar and find the hottest guy and target him. I became a hunter and I prided myself on being very good at it. I even got off on going to straight bars and developed a few very effective techniques at bagging straight guys too. This is a common way of approaching the situation and many gay men go their whole lives this way and it works out perfectly. After all, who came up with this whole monogamy, sex-love thing anyway? Wasn't that set up primarily as a means to keep the family genealogy intact? With male to male sex that isn't an issue, so why play by heterosexual rules? So I put sex on one shelf and love on the other and it all seemed to work just fine. Then some things began to change. Many of the super-hot guys I was playing with ended up being a big disappointment in bed or left me feeling hollow or empty after the sex was over. Sometimes the sex itself became more of a mechanical act than anything else. Something was missing and I couldn't put my finger on it. I wanted more of a connection but what?

Over time I came to see that quality far outweighed quantity. So I developed a circle of friends with fringe benefits.

However, people come and people go and I still didn't have an answer to this nagging "connection question" I had running around in the back of my head. Could it be love? No, I told myself because I had already been in a couple gay relationships and gotten my feet wet. It may be part of it but there was something else. It was like an energy exchange. It was intense and there was no mistaking it when it was present. The crazy thing was it wasn't always there with the same sexual partner all the time. Sometimes I would experience it with a one night stand. What was this connection or energy exchange all about?

How could I find a way to recreate it? Is it possible to see it in another before having sex? It was like catching the wind.

I then decided to go down one of the two roads most people don't like to talk about at parties. One is Politics and the other Religion. People have very strict comfort zones and the topic of religion usually turns some folks away. That's "ok" I'm just relating my story or path. If you don't agree with it, that's fine, everyone's path is different. Life would be pretty boring if everyone felt and thought exactly alike. We wouldn't have anything to talk about. So please keep an open mind and heart as I continue in sharing my quest in finding answers.

Well, the first thing I did with this religion puzzle was to check out what everyone had to offer. After all, I was an airline employee for many years and had access to the world so I took full advantage of it. It also gave me some great opportunities to take a taste of the local male flavors whenever possible.

This also gave me a good perspective of the local's cultural and sexual beliefs at the same time. What did I find? Well, after much searching I found that most religions reminded me of spokes of a large wheel. They all had the same base with separate approaches to the same central goal. The base was just a set of universal truths that were accepted by all. Once I saw this I started to ask questions.

It's funny but one afternoon I was watching a comedian on TV and he said something that made me smile. It went like this; "Religion was like going to the dentist as a little kid.

When he was little he went to the dentist and they drilled into his head and crammed stuff in there. He really didn't have a choice. Religion is like that. Now that you're an adult, you have a choice. You can drill that shit out!"

I guess what I'm trying to say is that you have a choice as an adult between what's irrational material and what brings you inner peace. To put it simply, take out the trash. That's what I did and shifted from being associated with any religion to being spiritual. I think they all have many valuable things to offer and some things that aren't. The first thing this shift accomplished was freedom of guilt about my sexuality and how much I wanted to have or with whom. Being spiritual left me only accountable to myself and God as I choose to relate to him/her on any given day. It also led me to look deeper into these universal truths and how they related to this question regarding "the connection" or "energy exchange." I started asking the questions of what works and what doesn't, why and what does it mean?

Psychology was my friend in college, so I went there next.

I read books regarding relationships. I started with authors like Leo Buscaglia and strange coincidences started happening. For instance the day I was reading one of his books while working a flight back from Hawaii. I was just sitting in a galley after the main service was done taking a break when the first class flight attendant came in and, seeing what I was reading, asked me if Leo had signed and given it to me. I asked her what she was talking about and she said he was up in first class at the moment. She then suggested that I go and get it signed while I had the chance. I went up to visit him just before landing and we talked briefly while he signed the book for me. The thing that really blew me away was the fact that he waited at the gate until everyone got off the flight. We sat alone in the empty gate area for almost an hour discussing his book and the concepts of loving and relating. This was truly an unexpected gift. The chain of odd events continued with people popping into my life who had just the right books at just the right time. One day I was sitting on the couch watching a PBS show featuring Dr. Wane Dyer. He was speaking about this connection thing I had questions about and then mentioned a chapter strongly influenced by his dear friend Leo Buscaglia.

That did it. I had to get the book! That evening I had an overnight in Washington and oddly enough there was a bookstore across the street from my hotel. I went in found the book and brought it up to the counter. The women there looked at me in shock and said, "How did you get this? It's been out of stock for weeks." I just smiled, shrugged and bought the book. Not only did the book answer many of the questions regarding this "connection thing" but also referred me to a few other books which offered helpful perspectives.

I not only looked at the spiritual side of the equation but also took a hard look at quantum physics and any relationship it may play in all this. Much to my surprise it proved to have many answers. If you want a taste of what I'm talking about try renting the DVD titled "What the Bleep Do We Know!?" (20th Century Fox Home Entertainment, 2005).

Just remember, quantum physics is a real rabbit hole and you have to ask yourself how far down you really want to go. Dr. Hawkins in his book "Power vs. Force" had some profound views regarding patterns and order in what may appear at the surface as random events. But, what really caught my eye was his view on energy calibrations in people.

I finally had the main pieces to the puzzle I was working on. Now it was just a matter of figuring out how to make them all fit. So I asked myself again, "Why can't the two be one again?" Sex, love, and this exchange of sexual energy in a BD/SM setting. I found the road toward being able to enjoy this intense type of experience on a more regular basis.

At this point my thinking shifted completely. I was now able to have an intense sexual experience with someone I just met or someone I've known for years. It was just a matter of being able to spot the right opportunity when it presented itself. Also knowing there are no coincidences, just the illusion of coincidence. The idea is to transition from an "I want" or "I need" mindset to "what can I give in this moment." This is a big school ground and we're all here to teach each other. When you give you receive.

Everyone has their own flavor or expression of this sexual/ spiritual energy and different people are attracted to you at different times. When you understand this you see the people who spring up in your life at the right moment and are able to identify them. When you reach this point experiencing the sexual/spiritual connection will be commonplace. Sex and love are reconnected and any feeling of being hollow after a sexual encounter will be a thing of the past. Intensity is the order of the day and the comfort of knowing there is no need or rush for sex because you're not looking for it out of need. You're just grateful for what you already have no matter what form it comes in. After all, you always have choices and can pass on any given opportunity if you want to.

Well, if you're made it this far you've been waiting for the "Big" answer to the question. What is this sexual energy?

You may even have a few more questions like; How do I find it? How does it work? Will I know when the right opportunity presents itself or will I just be disappointed again?

As I mentioned before, everyone's path is different just as my induction into the BD/SM Fetish world is uniquely mine.

So too, you're path will be uniquely yours. Therefore your answers will be different. However, one thing is certain: you must always look into yourself for the answers. With that in mind, the answers I found are:

- The "connection" is an exchange of energy between two souls.

- It's a by-product of being fully present in the moment in a state of sharing, no matter what the level of intensity of play.

- You know it when you feel it. It's a deep feeling of passion that's like electricity in the air no matter how short lived the experience or scene. Once felt, you want it again and again.

- Opportunities are all around you in every moment. However, the question you need to ask yourself is: Why am I not seeing them for what they are instead of what I want them to be?

- Shift your focus. It's no longer an issue of quantity but rather quality and connection.

Well, you've gotten your first glimpse of what it feels like to re-merge your sex, love and spirituality. The search for the higher self and to encourage it in others is not an easy path but one with great rewards. Remember, we're here for each other so we can learn and grow not because we're so fabulous.

Once you understand this, all your relationships will improve.

You're primary relationship is with yourself and the Universe/ God as you see him/her on any given day. Life is a big school and each relationship is an opportunity to grow and learn, and everyone learns. So take what you want from this chapter and move on. That's all you need to do.

Chapter 7: The Link in the Chain

Passing on the Legacy

This subject holds a special meaning for me because of my personal life experience. The reason for this is because of the time frame in which I "came out" as a gay male and as a Leatherman. Yes, I'm talking about the devastation of AIDS.

There aren't many of us left, and the ones that are don't seem to be taken very seriously anymore. Why? The answer is easy. Many in the generation that have followed may think of it as the past because they haven't lived through it. They haven't lost anyone close to them as a result. As I mentioned before: in this day and age, we have all sorts of medications to combat the virus, so it doesn't seem as if it's a life or death issue. It's more of an inconvenience where you'll just need to take some pills to manage. Besides, they're coming out with better stuff every day, "Right?"

True, if you haven't lived through something, how are you expected to relate to it? I can understand that train of thought. I can also understand the advances with modern medication, but let me tell you, the fight isn't over yet. Don't fool yourself.

This was just a wake-up call. I don't want to seem like the Harbinger of Doom, but who knows what your generation could be dealt? With that thought in mind, let me tell you about your importance in the "Big Picture."

First of all, I'm going to need to give you a little history lesson. Back in the mid-70's the Leather, BD/SM, and Fetish communities were in their "heyday." Even though it existed as a subculture, it was very alive, healthy and flourishing. When AIDS entered the scene this subculture was shunned as the black sheep or scapegoat of the gay community. After all, their sexual habits were way outside of the sexual norms of even the main stream gay community. Which, by the way, were already on the hot plate at the time. Most of the Old Guard Leathermen went into hiding with their boys to wait out the storm. Little did they know the storm would last so long. In the beginning the devastation was quick and merciless, many died in just a few months. The gay male population in San Francisco alone dropped 70% in the mid- to late-80's because of it. It's sad; I actually got accustomed to the fact that there wasn't a month that went by when I'd be attending a memorial for one friend or another. All the while the leather/fetish community was getting a lot of the bad press because their sex practices were viewed as highly unsafe.

I guess I couldn't have picked a worse time to come out of the closet and deal with being gay, let alone coming to terms with my desire to explore my Leather Fetish curiosities.

When I came out there wasn't a reliable AIDS blood test. There definitely wasn't any medication available. No-one knew for sure how it was transmitted either. I looked at it as a horrible game of Russian roulette every time I had a sexual encounter.

If you got it, then it was "at best" five years before you died of some horrific illness. Most of us saw the many terrible faces of death it presented because of the friends we'd visited in the hospital before they passed. People you once recognized were now all covered in legions or totally wasted away. It was horrific.

However, there's a famous saying, "That which does not kill us makes us stronger."

It seems as if it became a general mindset for those of us not willing to give in or lie down and die. Many tried their best and still died but some of us still remain. Sometimes I still ask myself why I was so lucky.

So where does this leave us? Well let's come back to the present and our current dilemma. One thing that I've observed is the disappearance of the ugly side of AIDS. By this I mean most of the men the current generation sees are all healthy looking and pumped up on steroids. It almost glamorizes being infected. Don't kid yourself. Taking steroids is just one of many little chess moves to counter the horrible side effects of HIV medications. The most common of cause is wasting. Steroids are just one of the things to help a person suffering from lipodystrophy (or wasting away) to keep it at bay. Just because someone looks great doesn't mean it's easy to manage. There's also something else. Because of the past circumstances we're left with a big hole or break in the passing of knowledge from one generation to the next.

The remaining Old Guard that survived are too old for the tastes of the new and upcoming generation.

This new generation might be interested in someone in their 30's or 40's but rarely someone in their 50's, 60's and above.

You can't blame them; it's just what they like.

This left us with a break in the chain or lifeline that passed forward the hands-on experience from one generation of Leathermen to the next. Not everyone was wiped out of course. The ones that survived were hard to find or too busy fighting the battle to raise charity money, caring for the sick or were just too burnt out to invest much energy into full-time training. There were exceptions of course, but considering the high mortality rate, they didn't have a huge impact. Many times it was the generation which they trained that died. Such was the case with my generation and it wasn't pretty. So what happened, the next generation which followed had low to no male to male interaction regarding leather male bonding, trust or the traditions and rituals that went with it. Sadly they had to resort to archived books, B/D S/M fetish publications, porn or instructional videos.

Now I have to say, books are knowledge and knowledge is not to be taken lightly. Otherwise I wouldn't be taking the time to share my life and views of all this with you. So by all means, please read and read as much as you can. What I am saying is; hands-on experience carries with it the crucial message of trust and intimacy that books and stories can't. Life is meant to be experienced, not lived out vicariously through books, the Internet or television. That's why so many youth of this generation had a hard time bridging the gap between the story book fantasy scene world that they read about and the real world issues of relationships that came along with it.

The current generation is going through materials and movies as best they can to recover what was lost or what they feel is missing. They're desperately looking for answers to the questions only human touch and contact can offer. I think they're doing a great job considering what they have to work with. However, the void still left its mark. It was very common to see people experiencing many theatrical play scenes and not experience any significant connection with anyone.

True living is through fully experiencing things for yourself.

This life is "your story." Therefore you get to pick who is in it and what part each person plays, but it's not going to happen if you don't go out there and act on what you've read, seen in movies or tried to experience through a computer screen. You have to live it.

I'll tell you a little story to give you an example of what "living it" is like. Getting close to another male has many ways of expanding your horizons. On this occasion, I was visiting Palm Springs and ran into a hot Daddy friend of mine named Dale.

This was a man's man, and he towered over me. On the night in question, I ran into Dale at the local leather bar where he worked. He was off duty and asked me to join him. One thing led to another, and before I knew it, we were French kissing so heavily that I thought my eyes were going to get sucked out of my skull. He was strong and forced himself on me repeatedly. I put up enough resistance to make it interesting and heated.

As we made out, I thought in the back of my mind, "Man, this guy can really salivate!" Just then, Dale grabbed the back of my neck and pulled our heads apart. At the same moment he squeezed the back of my neck hard enough to get a reaction.

I opened my mouth and was about to say "What the fuck!" but never got the chance. As soon as my mouth was open Dale spat in it. I was stunned and froze like a block of ice, but before I could fully register what had just happened, Dale lunged in with another kiss and scooped it out. After a moment Dale could still sense my rigid body and pulled off. He looked me dead in the eye and said, "What... you swap spit all the time when you're kissing so, what's the big deal?" 'True,' I thought. What Dale had said made perfect sense. I just never thought about it that way. I have to admit; it was very hot and had great shock value. This was my first induction into raunchy kissing, and I liked it. There were other things that followed, like shared breathing and breath control, but they came later.

So what does the new millennium have in store for us?

Growth is one thing that's very evident. There are so many young men and women starving for the opportunity to explore this wondrous new world of sexual diversity. I'm overloaded with boys who want a Mentor or Guide. There's a huge influx of newcomers that need to be guided. Mostly it's for their safety. Safety is a big issue, and it's the topic of my next story.

This story has special significance because it was the event that caused me to become a Mentor.

It all started when I happened across my old friend Graylin T. Our friendship is eternal, and we always pick up from where we've left off, even if it's been years since the last visit. Graylin asked me why I haven't started to train boys again. I said I never really thought about it even though the reason I stopped was no longer relevant. Besides, I didn't think there was much need for it these days. Graylin advised me that it was more important than ever. He said that everything the Old Guard taught me would be lost if I didn't pass it along. I thought it was a pretty good pitch, but I wasn't buying it. I figured there were plenty of other qualified men out there who could do the job.

I was too busy. However, deep down inside, I knew my friend was right. Then something happened that changed everything:

One night while I was attending a Southwest Regional Leather competition, I witnessed something that compelled me to return. I call this story "The boy and the flogger." The story begins on "Meet-and-Greet Night" when all of the out-of-town judges and guests arrive and meet at one of the local bars to spend some time together before their official duties really kick in the following evening. I arrived early and chatted with the owner of the new leather store. The owner was new and had no previous experience making or selling leather, so I wanted to see what he had to offer. One item caught my eye. Not because I liked it but because I thought it was dangerous. He had taken a series of telephone cables and made them into a flogger. The cables had been split open to expose all of the multi-colored wires for the whipping section of the flogger. The part that concerned me the most was the fact that the ends of the cables had been stripped so that the naked metal wire was exposed. This clearly was a toy for the more advanced player and was made to rent flesh. Aside from the out-of-town guests, this was not the sort of toy to be displayed in a bar that hosted novices "for the most part." This is when I made my first mistake. I raised an eyebrow then put it back and didn't say anything. After all, there were some heavy players coming to the bar that weekend and one of them may want it. I moved on and started to mingle with everyone as they arrived.

At one point I was engaged in a very intense conversation with a longtime Leather brother named Chris R. We had known each other many years, and I had even been one of his judges when he ran for my old regional Mr. Drummer title. He didn't come down from Las Vegas very often, so we always made the best of our time whenever we got the chance. While we were talking, a boy came racing up and cut into our conversation.

He'd seen the flogger attached to my side and said with great excitement, "I want you to flog me!" You could tell by the look in the boy's eyes that he had no time to wait and just wanted the thrill of the moment. I stopped my unfinished sentence with Chris and turned to the boy. I said very nicely that I would be more than happy to discuss this with him if he would simply wait a moment while I finished the conversation with my friend.

With an exasperated huff, the boy ran off into the bar. I made a mental note to go and look for him after my conversation was finished. But alas, I never got the chance. Just a few minutes later, I caught out of the corner of my eye, the boy bent over the bar being flogged by someone I'd never seen before. Yep, you guessed the worst of it. He was being flogged by the very flogger I had been concerned about at the beginning of the night! I excused myself from

Chris and went right over, but by the time I made it across the crowded room, it was done. It only took a few badly placed swipes to quickly end the scene.

By the time I got to the boy the person flogging him was gone and just the boy remained. My first thought was 'Damn! A Broken Toy!' He was hunched over the bar with his head in his hands. I came up to him and asked him if he was "ok". He looked up at me with tears in his eyes and said, "I thought this Leather-Fetish thing was supposed to be fun and cool. I guess I was wrong." I took my cool beer bottle and placed it on the gash across his neck and said, "I'm sorry this happened to you. The BD/SM Fetish experience is a lot of fun. You just had a bad experience. Please don't let it stop you from giving it another try. If it's done right, it's an incredible experience." I stayed with him for a while then said, "One more thing, if you ever want to be flogged again, always go to someone who has their own flogger and always ask them to demonstrate how they use it on an inanimate object, like the back of a chair before taking a single stroke on you." He nodded his agreement, and I told him that he could come over and spend more time talking with me if he wanted and went back to Chris. He was a very handsome boy and so full of life and energy. Because he was so impatient, it cost him dearly. Then again, at that age so was I. The only difference was that I had someone around to make sure I didn't become just another "Broken Toy." In that moment Graylin's words finally hit home.

From that day forward I made a personal commitment to become a Mentor.

It's strange, but when you're overloaded with sudden growth accompanied by a lot of inexperienced people, safety suddenly becomes a very important issue. Of course, there are other things in store for us.

Change is another, considering how well humans adapt to changing environments. We can't expect them to take all of the Old Guard rituals they've read about and just repeat them, especially if they don't agree with them. This process would have happened anyway; it's just that one particular event made it happen at a much faster pace. After all, nothing stays the same. Many of the rules as we knew them are out the window. Let me share with you a few stories which I hope will shed some light on the subject. Besides, I'd like to give you an example of how views and traditions change from one generation to another.

This story I call "The story of the boy, Old Guard, and the Statue of Liberty."

Way back when I was a regional Mr. Drummer I had a boy counterpart that competed with me. This boy was very progressive in his manner and his views, especially when it came to the topic of the Old Guard. It was as if he didn't have much use for them or their opinions. On the other hand, many of the judges that year were Old Guard. They were much too old for his liking and he didn't want any of their advice. Therefore, he didn't go out of his way to show them any respect and got a lot of resentment for it. However, he was very intelligent and when anyone debated him on a subject he almost always had a very sound and valid basis for his rebuke.

On one particular occasion, he got into a debate with a very intelligent member of the Old Guard regarding the respect the Old Guard had earned. The boy presented an analogy to demonstrate his view of the situation as the new generation who would be replacing him. He said the Old Guard and the new generation that would follow are like the Statue of Liberty.

The Old Guard was the support structure of hard steel beams and ugly old rusty supports. They were not very pretty to look at but were vital to holding it together. They symbolize the rigid old rules and a great deal of the money which was being pumped into the community to keep it going through its events and businesses. However, they were too old and unattractive to be seen or admired anymore. The young generation was the outside of the statue with all its beautiful curves and lines. A symbol for all to see and enjoy however, one cannot survive without the other. Who would want to look at a statue made of old rusty beams? Then again, a beautiful statue without support would be just a bunch of curved lines scattered all over the ground.

He said it's not that he didn't respect the Old Guard; he just didn't have any interest in them because they were too old to be attractive to him. If he didn't call someone Sir or Master as their title implied it was only because they were not "his" Sir or Master. It was a title that was earned by those who shared that type of relationship with him/her, so he didn't feel obligated to use such titles with people he didn't know.

He understood the fact that he would be missing out on what might be some incredible learning experiences but not at the cost of doing it with someone who didn't turn him on. After all, his generation would be taking their place anyway so what did it matter?

You may or may not agree with the boy's point of view; however he does have the final say, because he will be taking your place after you're gone unless you do something to change it. Ponder that for a while.

So how did what was missing in the "male bonding experience" impact the generations that didn't experience it?

One thing I've been hearing over and over again is a simple lack of etiquette or manners. For instance, someone toying a potential play partner along on the Internet only to coldly blow them off without a second thought before hooking up with them. After all, who cares if they've confirmed they're coming over? They've never really seen the person or know them face to face so why bother calling to cancel. "It's just a trick." Promoting etiquette and manners is one of the facets associated with this male bonding experience. Let me tell you a few more stories in the hope of enlightening you.

The next story is about a contest I attended many years ago. I was a boy and my Daddy at the time was a judge at the contest. However, it's not the Daddy that's the focus of this story but rather one of the judges on the panel. It all started at the beginning of the event with introductions. We were making the rounds saying hello to all of the judges and event staff. As we went through the crowd, I noticed a very handsome, well-kept, silver-haired man. He had a very nicely trimmed beard and he looked very much like a well put together polar bear-type guy. My Daddy spotted him in the crowd and went over to say hello. As we approached I noticed something that took me completely by surprise. As soon as we got within three feet of him the air was permeated with the smell of moth balls! It was so strong that it made me nauseous. It was sad to think that this man made so many efforts to look good as well as having an extremely kind manner, just to have it all ruined by the overpowering stench cloud which hovered around him. He must have stored his leather vest in a trunk full of moth balls all year. It just so happened, he was one of the judges and would be seated next to us at the judges table. I sat beside him all night and was forced to endure it. The only thing that kept running through my mind was the thought that they pulled "him" out of moth balls to judge the contest. It was sad. You couldn't say anything because there was nothing he could do about it. It would only make him feel self-conscious.

Besides, I was in full boy mode and I would have been totally out of place to say anything. In that moment I made myself a promise. I would make sure I took good care of my leathers so I would never end up like poor Judge Moth Balls. Had I not been given the proper training in good manners and etiquette, I may have embarrassed Judge Moth Balls and my Daddy at the same time.

Another topic I'd like to touch upon is taking pride in one self and your appearance. It sounds like a simple concept but carries a heavy meaning. This isn't a matter of being conceited or overly preoccupied with your appearance but rather an acknowledgement that you care for your body and see that it is well groomed. Anyone with a military back ground or civil service such as a policeman or fireman will relate to this. For those that don't, I'll tell a few stories to shed more light on the subject.

The next story is about my dad. He was a police officer in a small town back in New England. Back then policeman took great pride in their uniform and made great efforts to be presentable while on duty. As a way to make a little money on the side my dad use to have me polish and shine his black policeman's boots. He gave me explicit instructions on just how to do it including the small details like using a tooth brush were the top was stitched to the sole. I was well equipped with two types of buffing brushes and a buffing rag. The ironic part of all this was the fact that the polishing supplies where down in our musty basement with its dungeon like concrete and field stone walls. Just the same, I didn't think anything of it while focusing on the task at hand. When I was finished, I'd always bring them up to my dad for inspection. I took great pride in polishing those boots. He also made me feel good because even though he may have offered a suggestion or two from time to time, he never sent me back to do them over. To this day I always admire the look of a Leatherman in a pair of well-kept boots.

This brings me to something on a similar note. I feel the best way to take pride in the leather one has is by earning it. Earning one's leather is an Old Guard tradition and I feel it has a very sound basis in its conception. Sure you can go out and buy leather off the rack and it will make you feel good.

You'll feel even better if you have it custom made, but the top of the satisfaction scale is earning it. I'll tell you why by sharing a story about boy Jeremy and how he earned his first leathers. Unfortunately, one of the members of the local leather community had issues with boy Jeremy, because he didn't have any leather. I explained that leather is very expensive and a young boy such as he could not afford such pleasures when he was just starting out. Besides, earning one's leather is a more traditional and fulfilling way of acquiring it. There's also the old saying that "A Leatherman wears his leather in his heart," but I'll get back to that a bit later.

So where to start? Most Old Guard traditions start with boots, belt, an arm- or wrist-band, and a vest. It just so happened, I had a wonderful new pair of black leather lace up boots that were just his size. I had Jeremy show up at my place and told him in advance that he would be earning his first piece of leather. When he arrived I had the boots displayed in a very prominent place so he could lust over them. I first took him through what both of us would consider a very usual sexual encounter. We took a small break and my phone rang.

I answered it and, much to my surprise, it was another Daddy asking me what I was up to. I said I was in the process of bestowing a pair of boots on my boy if he properly earned them. The Daddy on the other end of the line asked if he had made it yet. I said in a voice loud enough for the boy to hear, "He's earned one boot but not the other. He'll really have to work for that one." With that, I hung up the phone and turned it off for the evening. I then took one of the boots and placed it in the middle of the living room table. I then said to the boy, "Well, I guess you're really going to have to show me how much you want this second boot. You can't go around with only one."

I instructed him to climb up on the bed, and I went into my closet and brought forth my "play bag." boy Jeremy was very curious to see what was in the bag, so the first thing I did was dump the contents on the middle of the bed. None of the items in it were familiar to him. I explained some of the items but didn't want to turn this into an all-night toy box discussion. What I really wanted was a series of cock rings which were at the bottom of the bag. boy Jeremy mentioned earlier that he wanted to experience cock and ball torture (CBT) for a short period, and tonight was going to be his big night.

There were many things I wanted to do with him but wanted to take him slow by introducing him to a seven gates cock ring experience. Although I only had five rings to work with and a lot of leather shoe lace type straps, I took him for one hell of a ride. He loved the sensation of having his cock all bound up. The weight of the steel cock rings at the base of his dick made his shaft throb with delight. He also was turned on by the masculine look of the bulging veins. I held his climax off as long as I could. He finally hit his peak when I was tugging on the ends of the leather straps wrapped around his balls while working over his nipples. The surge was impressive to say the least, and the boy immediately collapsed into a state of exhausted satisfaction. I pulled myself up close against his quivering body and firmly grabbed his crotch in one hand while rolling my arm under his head with the other.

I gave him a deep passionate kiss and informed him that he'd earned the other boot. Jeremy's grin stretched from one end of the room to the other. He was so proud of those boots. For a great deal of time afterwards, it was hard to catch him wearing anything else. By wearing them, some of the lingering memory of how he earned them could be re-lived, a special shared moment between a Mentor and his boy.

So now what do you think? Would you say that having something like boy Jeremy's experience is better than going into a store and picking out a good deal? Do you think there's a chance he'll take better care of those boots over others he had no personal connection with? What about the male bonding experience associated with the leather?

(A little side note, I'd been holding onto those boots, because they came from a dear friend and fellow Leatherman who'd passed away. I told his Daddy when I bought them at a silent auction that I would make sure they would be passed on to another worthy young Leatherman. The promise was kept and the bonding continues.)

I hope you enjoyed these stories about earning one's leather and taking pride in its care. You see, you can read about taking pride of your leathers, but living the experience makes the points sink in more deeply. That's another reason why the male bonding element is so important.

Now let's get back to wearing leather in one's heart. This is the most noble of virtues a person can have. It's so easy to spot, but like all other things in life, you need to take the time to look. It's simply the person who personifies what I described a Mentor or Guide to be. You've already read about them. I saw it in Walter as a "Quiet Confident Charisma." Now you can see it too, because you know what you're looking for. The most valuable Mentor/Guide is the one who holds their leather in their heart, because it's always with them. It's part of who they are, rather than what they wear. This point weighs heavily on me, because I have been very close to some of the finest men and women I've had the pleasure of knowing and calling my friends. All of them wore their leather in their heart. It's funny, but many people get confused when they see someone without leather. They'll be standing in a leather bar or some other leather venue and think they're not into the BD/SM fetish scene. This is a big mistake and has cost many a young boy a ride they'll never forget.

There are many situations when someone may refrain from wearing their leathers. Some players are just drawn to men dressed in leather but don't care to wear it themselves. Others are part of the different fetish subgroups – such as latex – and find leather locations to be the best place to find play partners. Whatever the reason, never underestimate someone because they're not wearing leather. Take the time to talk to someone of interest, and you'll soon find out what he/she is really all about. Most of the time it's just a simple change in your attitude or personal view of the person that makes all the difference.

As far as attitudes go, they're always changing and so do the rules and rituals that go along with them. It's the generation that follows that decides what stays and what goes. That's why it's so important to become one of the links in the chain which pass along this valuable information. After all, a chain is only as strong as its weakest link. All you have to do is make a choice. Are you going to sit it out or decide to make a difference? The choice is yours.

Now I would like to share an additional chapter with you, complements of author and good friend Andrew Cline. He touches on some aspects of the Daddy/boy relationship that I found extremely valuable. I found this chapter fascinating and couldn't put it down once I started reading it. I particularly enjoyed the section on the transforming power of role play.

Chapter 8: The Tender, Affectionate, and Verbal Daddy Type

----

by Andrew Cline

At a bar called the 440 in the Castro district of San Francisco, I had the great pleasure of discussing with Blade T. Bannon his second edition of this eye-opening book. Although Blade's breakthrough work rightly focused on Daddies in the BDSM community, I mentioned to him that there is another kind of a Daddy – the tender, affectionate and verbal Daddy. As Blade and I discussed this type of Daddy, Blade suggested I contribute a chapter to the second edition. In Blade's book, there are many scenes of great tenderness and affection given and received as After Care for a BDSM scene. This supplemental chapter covers scenes that start with and sustain tenderness and affection.

"I Love You, Daddy"

I'd been chatting online with a 28-year-old man who had fantasies about Daddy/boy role play. He lived about 250 miles away. On my way home from another trip, I was going to be in his neighborhood, so we had a chance to hook up. In our chat, he had mentioned one of his fantasies was to kiss and cuddle "in our undies." Once we were alone in our private room, we kissed and cuddled. He was eager to undress me and peel off his clothes, but I kept us in our undies. I pulled us onto the bed with me on my back and him on my chest, safe and warm in Daddy's arms. He looked up at me beaming and blurted out, "I love you, Daddy." Without hesitation I replied, "Daddy loves his boy!" Then, a sheepish look washed over his face. "I'm sorry, Daddy, but I accidentally just came." With an ear-to-ear grin on my face I said, "That's okay, son, at your age you'll be ready to go again in 20 minutes."

Daddy Means Many Things

I'm the first to say there is no single LGBT culture, but there are many things that are part of our collective experience, enough things that make us distinct from the predominant cultures around us. For example, David Nimmons, in his most excellent book "The Soul Beneath the Skin: Unseen

Hearts and Habits of Gay Men",[1] throws out a list of about 75 terms that most gay men know including the following dozen:

- Prince Albert

- fisting

- playdates

- backrooms

- flagging

- poppers

- ball stretchers

- frat games

- docking

- barebacking

- fuck buddies

- S/M runs

Nimmons says of these terms:

> Three things are worth noting. The first is many of us know much of what's on the list. It represents a widely shared pool of cultural knowledge. Second, most other folks don't share it, or even much care to. [Third,] these habits, opportunities, rituals, conventions, and language flourish entre nous [(i.e. between ourselves, in private)].

---

1   1st ed. N.p.: St Martin's, 2002. 80. Print.

Many remain largely unknown, even inconceivable, outside our clan.

He goes on to observe:

> What is key here is that in gay lives so many of these practices are accepted and known. They have a wholly different cultural centrality. In gay lives these acts and customs are not only conceivable, but common.

I bring up this sense of foreign culture because we also face the problem of translation. Non-gay people may know generally what words like "Daddy," "boy" and "son" mean in the erotic anecdote above, but they probably do not understand the context of consensual, safe, and sane kink. One of the reasons translations between one language and another are so difficult is that individual words usually represent a cluster of meanings. While it's possible to find a word in another language that is essentially the same, it is rare that the clusters of meaning overlap perfectly. When it comes to "gay culture," there are elements that need to be translated to non-gay people before they can understand them. So it is with the word "Daddy." For many (maybe even most) gay men, "Daddy" refers to a way a man looks, older and grayer. A hot Daddy emanates an air of sexuality about him because of his muscles and confidence; if he's well-endowed, so much the better. There are many, many Web sites that feature nude photos of men over 50 and the term "Daddy" is often used in the name or description of the site. However, the term "Daddy" is not defined only by appearance. It can and does refer to men of various ages who play the role of Daddy in a role play scene. (It can also refer to a lesbian woman playing the role of Daddy in a role play scene.)[2]

For most non-gay people, the word "Daddy" in English is an informal word for "father." Except in the Southern parts of the US, using the word "Daddy" for one's father is something that most people out-grow. However, the relationship between a father and son is one of the few same-sex relationships that non-gay society recognizes and even idealizes. A gay male couple with a significant age gap will often be assumed to be father and son by non-gay people. That happened to me and my late partner frequently. Late middle-aged cashiers at the hardware store, newcomers at church coffee hour, and even strangers we'd meet on vacation would often ask if we were father and son. This was despite the fact that I was nearly a foot taller and pounds heavier. One explanation for this mistaken identity is that non-gay people sensed and admired the depth of the relationship between us, but the only cultural reference they had was father and son.

The word "Daddy" can be imbued with layers of emotions and experiences for gay and non-gay people alike. The Urban Dictionary Web site allows people to record their own definitions of words. It's a treasure trove of modern usage – especially slang, jargon, and idioms. As with most dictionaries, definitions are presented with one or more example sentences. These example sentences shed great light on informal and slang usage. Multiple people can

---

2   Some of the erotic stories in the book "Doing It for Daddy" include lesbian role play scenes where the Daddy is female. This shows the power of fantasy over flesh. (Califa, Pat. "Doing It for Daddy." Alyson book, 1994.)

record definitions of the same word. The term "Daddy" has definitions recorded in Urban Dictionary as I write this.[3]

Of these 43 definitions…;

- 17 define "Daddy" for straight sexual relations (what females might call male partners without reference to age)…;

- 11 define "Daddy" as a male with some superior attribute (work supervisor or a man who is best at something)…;

- nine define "Daddy" in terms of fatherhood as a concept that transcends biology (a man who acts like a father to children he hasn't sired)…;

- three define "Daddy" for gay sexual relationships (two referencing age and one pointing out age is not relevant)…;

- two define "Daddy" in phrases that suggest some sort of twisted, illogical joke; these types of jokes are prevalent on Urban Dictionary…;

- one defines "Daddy" as prison slang for a male who uses other males for sexual release (that is, "active" versus "passive" sexually).

Although none of the definitions recorded for the word "Daddy" fully conveyed the richness of gay male Daddy/son role play, one is worth looking at more closely:

---

3   "Urban Dictionary: Daddy." Urban Dictionary. Web. Urban Dictionary allows readers to vote "Thumb Up" or "Thumb Down" on definitions, and this establishes the order in which definitions are numbered.

Daddy – A bisexual or homosexual man who is sexually attracted to younger men.[4] The term can be used affectionately or in sexual role playing. The Daddy is often paired with one Boy or more. Typically the Daddy is the more aggressive, dominant male of the two. Similar to "Sugar Daddy," age may or may not be relevant to the Daddy or boy.

Example Sentences:

- "Who's your Daddy?"

- "I'm a Daddy's boy."

- "I'm out looking for a Daddy tonight."

- "Will you be my Daddy?"

- "Oh, ooh, Daddy buy me that cock ring!"

There is a striking mismatch between the example sentences and the definition: four out of the five example sentences show that it's the younger men who are attracted to an older man. "I'm looking for a Daddy tonight" is more likely to be spoken by a younger man than an older man. Here is as good as any place to explain that the Daddy/son role play discussed in this book is of a fantasy nature only. Some people react very negatively to Daddy/son role play, because they fear it has something to do with sexual assault on minors or illegal sex with minors. The fantasy discussed in this book is between consenting adults. In my

---

4   That human males are attracted to youth is pretty basic to our species. The 1999 film "American Beauty" won five Academy Awards® (including "Actor in a Leading Role" and "Best Picture"), and the plot was about the mid-life crisis of a suburban father who is attracted to his highschool daughter's female friend. No one critized the movie for this basic plot element. It was accepted as very believable and common.

experience, "Will you be my Daddy?" is far more likely to be spoken by a man in his 30's than in his 20's. It takes a certain amount of emotional maturity to admit that one might want to explore the emotional landscape of Daddy/son role play. The Urban Dictionary definition does hit the nail on the head when it points out that age may not be relevant. One of the hottest and most honest amateur videos of a Daddy/son role play that I've ever seen involved a long-time couple in their mid-60's. One man acted the role of the boy and one man acted the role of the Daddy. The intensity of their emotions transcended their physical ages.[5]

Of course, not all men in their 50's and above accept the label "Daddy." Some quite strongly reject it for various reasons. Some men's self-image is still that of an 18-year-old "between the ears." Their aged and gray bodies do not reflect their inner joy of pursuing a zipless fuck. The phrase "snow on the roof, but fire in the hearth" is a fine metaphor for this. Other men are highly suspicious that younger men who want a Daddy may not be mature enough to carry their share of a relationship. Some men in their 20's and 30's are too clingy and dependent. It can be suffocating. Senior gay men in their 60's, 70's, and 80's often share cautionary tales of young men who are looking for financial support. These younger men are the predators, not the older men. Finally, many men seem to be commitment-phobic. Stepping up to the role of a Daddy is simply too much responsibility.

Most men who engage in Daddy/son role play want the fantasy, not actual incest. The thought of sex with one's

---

5   Slavery is illegal in most countries, yet few people think a consensual Master/slave BDSM relationship has anything to do with slavery or human trafficking. So it should be for consensual Daddy/boy role play. For absolute clarity, the Daddy/son role play described in this essay is of a fantasy nature only and between consenting adults.

actual biological father is often distasteful in the extreme. In my opinion, for most Daddy/son role play, the "Daddy" may be a surrogate of some sort, but there is also an element of transformation and re-creation that eliminates the anger, hostility, and conflict often present in actual father/son relationships. Daddy/boy role play usually involves lots of verbalizing feelings. Just using the taboo words "Daddy" and "boy" can be powerfully erotic. Some common Daddy/boy dialogue includes:

- "You're a Daddy's boy."

- "Good boy!"

- "Knees apart, son."

- "Did I do good, Daddy?"

- "Damn good, boy."

- "Cum for Daddy."

In addition to the "Daddy" role, an older man may be asked to re-enact and play other related fantasies:

- pastor or priest

- friend's dad

- sports coach

- scout master

I've had the intense experience on a few occasions of role playing the actual, estranged biological father. Since the 1960's, divorce has become completely de-stigmatized. This has left in its wake many men, both gay and non-gay, with profound abandonment issues. Role playing the biological father takes balls. It's delving into some pretty deep emotional territory. Even though it's "make believe," telling a man, "I'm sorry I left you and your mother," or "You were conceived in love, son, even though it didn't work out between me and your mother," is pretty heady stuff.

Finally, a multicultural Daddy will recognize, know, and use the right words for "Daddy" in other languages as needed: Papa, Baba, Abebi and many others.

The Transforming Power of Role Play

Some BDSM pursues the intensity of physical sensation. Similarly, fantasy role play can pursue the intensity of emotions, especially when we draw upon our own experiences and memories. These memories can include strongly felt desires that were never acted upon. The desire for affirmation and affection by our fathers is perhaps one such strongly felt desire. Both gay and straight men report troubled relationships with their fathers. The scholarly research conducted by Dr. D. Michael Quinn dispels these notions that only gay men have poor relationships with their fathers. Quinn writes:

> I also accept the research that indicates that human environment (including early childhood experiences, family culture, socialization, social class, and religion) "constructs" how people recognize, define, experience, and express their

inherent sexuality. However, I reject the claim of some therapists that male homosexuality is caused by a poor relationship between son and father, because such assertions are based on fallacies of evidence or interpretation.

For sixty years, various studies have demonstrated that a significant percentage, perhaps a majority of American males has always felt estranged from the fathers who raised them. As early as 1928, Meyer F. Nimkoff found that 60 percent of the 1,336 males he studied (average age 22) did not feel close enough to their fathers to confide in them, and the father-son relationship was distant in other significant ways. He concluded: "If sons withhold trust from their fathers, it appears they deny his leadership and limit association with him, also." Researchers have also noted that one-third to one-half of American teenage boys and adult men regard their fathers as "distant, unaccepting, cold or indifferent." The psychiatrist Irving Bieber found that 37 percent of the heterosexual males he studied even said they "hated" their fathers, which was paralleled by a study that 21 percent of male heterosexuals at the University of Utah disliked their fathers.

Unlike heterosexual men, gay men can create options and opportunities to reenact and transform their father/son relationships through creative role play. What if we had a father who accepted our sexuality? Who didn't shame us for our attraction to men? Who mentored us on the manly ways of seeking and fulfilling our sexual desires? Who taught us to enjoy and celebrate horniness and its release? Who was emotionally available, tender, and affectionate? That's the fantasy role play of a tender, affectionate Daddy.

Growth Occurs at the Edge

A man who offers himself as a tender, affectionate surrogate Daddy must have conquered many of his own negative feelings and experiences regarding the role of his father and father-figures in his own life. It almost goes without saying a man who has never taken on this challenge is unlikely to make a good Daddy. The psychologist Eric Berne, for example, in his therapeutic approach called "transactional analysis" theorized that we all have three basic ego-states: Parent, Adult, and Child. Much grief is caused in interpersonal relationships when we assume the ego-state of parent or child but should be in the ego-state of adult. Fundamental to Berne's approach to therapy is that we can decide our own stories and destinies. Unlike Berne, who thought the golden mean of psychological health was adults interacting with each other only in the adult ego-state, I believe age role play explores the sexual dynamic of the parent ego-state interacting with a child ego-state.

The child ego-state persists from our own experiences and history. Usually, the parent ego-state is internalized from our experience with our parents. Instead of trying to deny or suppress these internal ego states, one path to emotional health and freedom is to accept and transform these ego-states. That is to say, one can "re-program" the adult ego-state. If a person grew up with an alcoholic and philandering father, the internalized version of that parent ego-state can be replaced with an alternative, better parent ego-state. Likewise, a person who experienced emotional neglect and abuse can replace the frightened and angry child ego-state with a happier, more confident child ego-state.

In my own life journey, I've been helped along this path in two very powerful ways. First, when I was a man in my 30's, I had a wonderful Daddy. From him, I learned it was possible to receive the care and nurture of an older, wiser Mentor who was also a sexual Mentor. The emotionally bruised and physically battered child in me experienced care and nurture. I learned to care for my own inner-child. The T-shirt saying, "It's never too late to have a happy childhood," was made real for me in this experience.

Moreover, from this wise and older lover, I also learned to give care and nurture. The actual, internalized parents of my childhood were replaced by my becoming my own loving parent to myself first. This became the foundation for becoming a tender, affectionate Daddy to others. The cycle of dysfunction and abuse was replaced with the cycle of "good boy" becomes "affectionate Daddy" as I've aged. Simply put, now that I'm in my 50's, I can be a great Daddy because I once was a boy who had a great Daddy.

These two experiences resonate with approach offered by a type of 12-step meeting called Adult Children of Alcoholics (ACA). This group observes that relationships will be fundamentally flawed when a person is raised in a dysfunctional family. One of the basic tenants of ACA is, "The solution is to become your own loving parent." In particular, they say working the 12-steps of ACA will provide a key benefit: "You will become an adult who is imprisoned no longer by childhood reactions. You will recover the child within you, learning to love and accept yourself."[6] Being able to nurture and heal the inner-child of the past means I'm able to empathize with men who are still struggling with this. The clothes come off and there's hot sex, and it is in the context of a nurturing, mentor role play scene.

As it applies to Daddy/son role play, I would go so far as to say we can replace the internalized father of our childhood by being our own loving father to ourselves. As this relates to the psychological and sexual development of a gay male, we can replace all the shame and negative messaging of our youth with a celebration of sexual orientation and pleasure.

Many gay men have achieved a modicum of emotional freedom from their dysfunctional families by cutting off or limiting contact with their parents and siblings. The benefit of this cannot be denied. It's certainly better than being manipulated and continuing to suffer shame and false guilt. For many such men, this is all it takes to live a satisfying and happy life. Good for them. But, for those who find it still lacking, addressing the emotional needs of our inner-child and inner-parent can open avenues of increased joy and intimacy.

After sex, I have frequently had a cub fall asleep with his head on my fuzzy chest and my arms holding him safe

---

6   "The Solution - The Solution Is to Become Your Own Loving Parent." Adult Children of Alcoholics World Service Organization, Inc, n.d. Web.

and warm. It's a great feeling. True, a lot of men readily nod off after ejaculation, but this pattern also bespeaks of a special bond – one that feels good. It feels good to let go and let Daddy take care.

Sexual Re-Enactment of Assault, Trauma, or Abuse

Some men want an authoritarian or even abusive, humiliating Daddy. Some men want to combine the physical intensity of being a sub in a BDSM scene with the emotional intensity of Daddy/boy role play. To each his own. People who enjoy BDSM often look for a cause for their interest. While it's probably true that some men who want to play a boy had abusive fathers or father-figures in their childhood, there are just as many who didn't.

Daddy/boy role play can be a powerful tool for transforming our past experiences, but it's not a substitute for professional psychotherapy, 12-step programs, or coaching when role play is re-enacting adolescent trauma or abuse.

James Cassese's excellent book "Gay Men and Childhood Sexual Trauma: Integrating the Shattered Self"[7] manages to provide both solid academic research and accessible self-help for men who experienced childhood sexual trauma.   It would be impossible to accurately summarize this important work; however, I would like to point out a few key observations:

---

7   N.p.: Routledge, 2000.

- Sexual relationships with preadolescent minors are more accurately described as "assaults," because there are almost always explicit threats of harm if the secret is divulged (these threats can even be death threats).

- Both gay and non-gay men often feel deep conflict that they had a bodily, physical reaction of pleasure to sexual stimulation even though it was coerced.

- Whereas non-gay men are often tormented with the question "What was it about me that attracted my assailant?" gay men are often tormented with the idea that the abuse was "all my fault (because I have same-sex attraction)."

A man who plays a Daddy, Master, or other dominant role would be wise to scan for signs that a particular kink scene could be the re-enactment of trauma. For example, it's usually a "red flag" when a man requires drugs or alcohol for sex, there is intense shame and conflict felt after a sexual encounter, and/or increasingly frequent sexual encounters are arranged, but are less and less satisfying. Men who are more than a bit compulsive about pursuing a humiliating, dominant, and aggressive Daddy for role play may find it helpful to consider if they are re-enacting childhood trauma. If so, there is a fine self-help resource on the Web called "One in Six" at http://1in6.org/. Men looking for workshops and other resources related to this topic may find Joe Kort's Web site, www.joekort.com/, helpful.

Maturity and Intimacy

Elsewhere in this book, Blade Bannon makes the point that choosing a mentor or Daddy should be done carefully. He goes so far as to say when looking for a Daddy, one should look for a man who has some depth of spirituality and ethical maturity. The sex advice columnist Dan Savage puts the responsibility squarely on the shoulders of the older person. Savage refers to this as the "Campsite Rule" – a phrase borrowed from Scouting – and applies it to younger/ older relationships: Leave the younger person better than you found him. The Wikipedia article on Savage's column, "Savage Love," provides a concise description.

With regard to readers who are in relationships with a large age disparity, Savage promotes his Campsite Rule: at the end of the relationship, the elder partner should leave the younger in "better shape than they found them." This includes no diseases, no fertilized eggs, no undue emotional trauma, and whatever education that can be provided.[8]

"Education" in this context certainly includes many possibilities when it comes to sex, relationships, and love. Having had plenty of practice, an older man knows his way around real bodies and approaches sex more realistically than the ritualized performance sex seen in porn videos. Many a Daddy has had to teach a cub to stop mimicking the bedroom gymnastics of porn and express instead what their bodies want and need. My Daddy of yesteryear taught me to top; while I was in him, he said, "Just do what your dick

---

8   Savage, Dan. "Open It, Already." Savage Love by Dan Savage. Index
        Newspapers, LLC.Web.

wants." With more experience, also comes knowledge of a wider palette of things that are likely to please a partner. An older man may guess a cub wants his nips played with or chewed, but it's an educated guess. Since older men generally have less sexual urgency, they are more likely to spot things a younger partner doesn't really like and pay attention to indirect cues. An older man is typically more confident and doesn't hesitate to ask directly.

A man who plays the role of Daddy also has enough experience to know that any intense scene needs After Care. As mentioned before, holding a cub safe and warm while he falls asleep on your fuzzy chest can be as fulfilling as a shattering orgasm. (Certainly, any cub who has had a shattering orgasm deserves a Daddy to hold him safe and near, "Daddy's got you.")

Education from an older man also extends well beyond the bedroom, especially if the Daddy/boy experience moves beyond a one-time hook up into an on-going relationship. An older man typically is more aware of the world around him. He's socially, emotionally, and financially more experienced and can share those skills with a cub. His references to pop culture may be dated, but that makes him a great partner when playing Trivial Pursuit and Scene It?®. Older men tend to be more established in their lives and careers; they can offer a wealth of advice about difficulties younger men face in the work world. Older men also tend to be more independent from their parents. While it's often true that gay men of all ages have a special bond with their mothers, it's also true that an older man typically has more experience with managing the complexities of families, even when that means distancing oneself from family.

The Campsite Rule also means to me that a Daddy with any depth of spirituality and ethics knows when sex with a younger man should not be entertained. In this age of Internet and smart phone ubiquity, there are plenty of minors posing as adults on personal ads and chat apps. It's pretty easy to detect these and avoid them. There are, however, many younger adult men who find their popularity in bars/clubs is focused on their ass. The attention may be almost intoxicating (and, therefore, obvious why they pursue it), but a tender, affectionate Daddy knows that sex and love can be very different things. Sometimes the best thing a Daddy can do for a younger man is help him experience a connection with another man that doesn't involve sex. On several occasions, I have responded to younger men who approached me on chat sites/apps with: "You don't need a Daddy... You need a big brother." In my experience, about half the time I am dropped with no further contact. In the other half of the time, I'm afforded the opportunity to offer the hand of friendship and mentoring. In both cases, I would say the campsite rule has been honored.

The Path Ahead

If you are wondering how to become the Daddy or boy of someone's dreams, I highly recommend you go back and re-read this book. Carefully observe your feelings and reactions to the scenes and ideas presented. Use this as a guide to consider what kind of Daddy or boy is most exciting and attractive to you. Also carefully evaluate those things you found squicky; those may be the very stepping stones that will take you to higher and better experiences. Every man has the opportunity to cultivate and develop the best attributes and aspects of his humanity. We do not have to merely accept the internalized version of our biological father or remain locked in unresolved childhood issues. We have the freedom to take on a healthy paternal instinct when we want to be the Daddy, and we also get the amazing chance of a "do over" if we want to play the devoted, loyal, and good son.

I'd like to thank Andrew once again for his contribution to this addition. I think you can understand why I found it valuable.

In closing, I'd like to say something to the potential Mentors out there. Mentors can be anyone. All you need to do is make it a primary focus in your life. It's very easy and takes less time than one might imagine. All you have to do is care. As for those looking for a Mentor or Guide, just look around, they're right in front of you. Be open and willing to learn new things and to trust. The rest, as they say, will take care of itself.

After Notes

I would like to take a moment to acknowledge some authors and their books. These pieces of literature made all the difference in making this book a reality. I would also like to take the time to describe some truths (or "golden nuggets") I found when reading them. If you find anything I say of interest, then please feel free to pick up a copy, and I'm sure you'll find some discoveries of your own.

- Townsend, Larry. "The Leatherman's Handbook." N.p.: L T, 1994. Print.

  Great beginner's book to look into the days of the Old Guard as they once were. The stories it told turned me on, and the history it conveyed I found inspiring. I highly recommend it.

- Baldwin, Guy. "The Ties that Bind." N.p.: Deadalus Co., 1993. Print.

  Great bridge book that transitions from the Old Guard to more modern times. Guy does an outstanding job of looking deeply into the many changing aspects of the BD/SM and Fetish lifestyles as we move into the future. He looks deeply into the dynamic of all different relationship types and breaks down many aspects of their functionality. He also offers some good sound advice. It's one book I've enjoyed reading on more than one occasion.

- Ruiz, Don M. "The Four Agreements: A Practical Guide to Personal Freedom." N.p.: Amber-Allen, 1997. Print. Toltec Wisdom.

  Waking from the dream of the planet, or the Mitote as Don Miguel puts it, is a hope I hold for everyone. I mentioned having conflicting voices in your head and how important it is to be at peace with yourself. This book addresses this subject perfectly as well as others.

- Buscaglia, Leo F., Ph.D. "Loving Each Other – The Challenge of Human Relationships." N.p.: Ballantine, 1984. Print.

  Leo Buscaglia does a great job of going into great detail in regard to aspects of showing verbal and nonverbal affection as well as important communication skills. He has a section regarding solicited advice that I always enjoy re-reading. He's also one of the authors I had the pleasure of spending some personal time with.

• Hay, Louise. "You Can Heal Your Life." N.p.: Hay House, 1984. Print.

There are many great life lessons in its pages. She presents lessons in self-love and self-healing, so you can extend love to anyone limitlessly. It's deeply spiritual and remarkably practical.

Louise Hay expresses the bond between sexuality and spirituality with clarity. She talks about multiple sex partners, bath houses, and other same-sex issues without losing focus how someone can still maintain a spiritual connection and inner peace. She worked very closely with AIDS patients and focused on how their attitude influenced their health.

• Hawkins, David R., M.D., Ph.D. "Power vs. Force." N.p.: Hay House, 1995. Print.

His presentation on power calibrations opened my eyes. I also enjoyed his presentation regarding order in things that appear random from a superficial view. He touches upon many of the universal truths I have been working with.

• Dyer, Dr. Wayne W. "The Power of Intention – Learning to Co-Create Your World Your Way." N.p.: Hay House, 2004. Print.

I already had the answers, but this book validated them in many ways. If your current search is leaning in more of a spiritual direction, then I suggest you give it a try. He's written many books, so you may find a subject that interests you. Just remember, as with all books, you may not agree with everything that's written in them. Just take what you want and move on.

- Williamson, Marianne. "A Return to Love – Reflections on the Principles of a Course in Miracles." N.p.: Harper Collins, 1992. Print.

- Williamson, Marianne. "A Course in Miracles." Harper Collins Audio Lecture Series. 1993. Lecture.

This is the one that gets you off the "What's-in-it-for-me?" mentality. You delve deeply into the real issues of the big pictures and relationships. If you're skittish with Christian verbiage and vocabulary, try to look past it or maybe try something else first. However, I highly recommend it.

Andrew Cline suggests the following two books:

- Nimmons, David. "The Soul Beneath the Skin: The Unseen Hearts and Habits of Gay Men." N.p.: St Martin's P, 2002. Print.

This is an amazing book that dismantles many false stereotypes that gay men have about themselves. We're more peaceful, charitable, and loving than non-gay people, and this can be demonstrated with serious social science research. We are also more creative when it comes to permissible intimacies. We allow ourselves a greater range of emotional and sexual expression, not only when it comes to BDSM and kink, but in virtually all aspects of our lives.

- Cassese, James. "Gay Men and Childhood Sexual Trauma: Integrating the Shattered Self." N.p.: Routledge, 2000. Print.

There is a profound difference between once being wounded and forever being damaged. There is a false notion that victims of childhood sexual assault are both "damaged goods" and destined to become perpetrators. The cycle can be broken and health and wholeness can emerge. One of the first steps is to end denial and self-blame. This book is intended as text book for psychological professionals; however, it is very readable and has a powerful message of hope and balance.

About the Author

Blade T. Bannon

Blade T. Bannon was originally born and raised on the East Coast, but entered the Leather and BD/SM communities in the early 80's while coming out in Los Angeles. He then moved to Austin, TX, where he continued his journey and later moved to Phoenix, AZ, where he settled for 17 years. It was there that he involved himself in the local and national Leather events. He has held multiple titles as a representative for the Leather BD/SM Community. Some of these titles include Bum Steer Drummer boy 1991, Mr. Charlie's Leather 1993 and Southwest Mr. Drummer 1993.

At the time the first addition was published he was holding the title of Arizona Mr. Leather Sir 2008.

Blade has devoted much of his time to the community in different ways. He's held many leadership roles which include the offices of Secretary, Vice-President and President of the Universal Brotherhood of the Leatherlords. He has volunteered his time and/or money to many charity organizations. Some of which include: Volunteers in Direct Aid (VIDA), Logan's Play Ground, Homeward Bound, Community Youth Center PHX, Meals-on-Wheels, Body Positive, MS150, Sisters of Perpetual Indulgence and many more.

Being an airline employee of many years, Blade has traveled to many places around the world. He's enjoyed spending time in the local Leather, BD/SM, and fetish culture in many of these places as well as experiencing their unique cultural diversity.

Blade now spends most of his time in San Francisco with his partner and extended Leather family. However, he still returns to Phoenix on a regular basis. When he's not traveling, he still actively Mentors young men and devotes any extra time he may have to the community at large.

www.ingramcontent.com/pod-product-compliance
Lightning Source LLC
Chambersburg PA
CBHW070800290326
41931CB00011BA/2087